Snippets From The Trenches
a mother's AIDS memoir

Cover photo: Taken by Gary Wagman of himself
Cover design by Freda Wagman

e-mail: freda.wagman@sbcglobal.net

FREDA
WAGMAN

SNIPPETS FROM
THE TRENCHES
a mother's AIDS memoir

2007

Snippets From The Trenches
a mother's AIDS memoir

CONTENTS

If I should die and leave you here a while
Be not like others, sore, undone, who keep
Long vigil by the silent dust and weep.
For my sake, turn again to life and smile.

Unnerving heart and trembling hand to do
That which will comfort other souls than thine.
Complete these dear unfinished tasks of mine
And I, perchance, may therein comfort you.

Mary Lee Hall

NOTE

For those who would ask why I didn't elaborate about the people I've written of, I would like to say that in trying to maintain the accuracy of the material, I have had to rely on whatever information is and was available. There were many people who appeared briefly in the seemingly never-ending procession during my tenure, whom I was able to help (or perhaps not) and move on to the next, or who died before there was more information to add to what I already had.

Hence, the title, *Snippets*.

It has been a long time since these events took place and there may be errors or inaccuracies, for which I offer my sincere apologies.

ACKNOWLEDGMENTS

Many people made this book possible, but very few are still here for me to thank.

For their willingness to allow me to include the experiences I shared with their loved ones, I am deeply grateful to Truman Dunahoo, Margaret and Bill Laderach, Jennifer and her mother (last names withheld at their request), and Tim's mother, who also asked that her name not be given, but told me she is proud be included.

To Stephen Hill, producer and announcer of the National Public Radio program *Hearts of Space*, for adding a great measure of purpose to my work with people living and dying with AIDS. Stephen also introduced me to the work of composer Constance Demby, who has graciously permitted me to quote from a letter she received from a physician regarding the powerful impact of her music on dying patients.

For allowing me to mention their visible presence and involvement in the candlelight march in 1983, I am grateful to The Sisters of Perpetual Indulgence in San Francisco.

Some of the colorful details were provided by John Paul Barnisch, an attorney who was one of the early AIDS Foundation Houston volunteers. He now serves as a judge in the City of Houston.

Sue Lovell, a Houston City Council Member, was instrumental in the initial formation of AIDS Foundation Houston and shared with me her knowledge of the earliest days of the organization, which I was able to piece together with other fragments of information I had about the structure of the foundation. Her initial interest began when her younger brother, Bobby, became ill and friends of his asked her to become involved. The basic preparation by Ms. Lovell and a small group of concerned therapists and physicians, motivated by a single individual whose unusual illness was brought to their attention, enabled the earliest volunteers to join the fledging group. Chapter 3 in this book is taken from my interview with Ms. Lovell, and I am deeply grateful to her for granting me permission to tell her part of the story.

A very important person in Gary's life was Thorn Coyle, whom Gary knew through his Sufi studies and turning practice. Gary was known in his Sufi group as Ram. Ms. Coyle has permitted me to close this book with a poem she wrote for him on the night he died. She is a musician, dancer, poet, and activist. To find out more about her teachings, her website is www.thorncoyle.com.

My manuscript readers—Susan Choi, Truman Dunahoo, and Ann Seward—have my heartfelt appreciation. Susan Choi's professional critique enabled me to bring the bud of my story to full bloom.

I was unable to locate family members or friends of some of the individuals whose stories are included in this book, in order to request permission to write about their loved ones. By telling their stories, my intention is to memorialize those loved ones, and to express my gratitude for having been allowed to be a part of their lives.

I am especially grateful for the knowledge and patience of Pressque Editing, and BookSurge editor, Emmy Eoff. Thank you both for your much needed help.

The encouragement to tell my story came from many

sources: my family, friends, and members of the Bering Spiritual Support Group in Houston, Texas.

To all of you, thank you so much.

THE ORIGIN

In 1981, the illness was called GRID, for Gay-Related Immune Deficiency. As the virus claimed one life after another, and realizing that it was affecting not only gay men, the name AIDS was designated, the acronym for Acquired Immune Deficiency Syndrome.

In 1983, Dr. Luc Montagnier, a French researcher at the Pasteur Institute in Paris, isolated the lymphadenopathy-associated virus, known as the LAV retrovirus. Meanwhile, Dr. Robert Gallo was working at the National Cancer Institute in New York, and in 1984 isolated what he called the HTLV III, or the human T-Cell lymphatropic virus III.

The Journal of the American Medical Association (JAMA), in 1986, determined that LAV and HTLV III were the same virus, and they were given the designation of HIV, or Human Immunodeficiency Virus.

The origin was irrelevant—people were sick and dying, and desperately needed help.

FOREWORD

My son, Gary, died twelve years ago. He had been diagnosed in 1983 with a strange illness from a then unknown cause. Shortly after his death, I was asked to speak to a gay student group at Rice University about how my life had been changed by AIDS, and was told that my remarks should not be too depressing. My first reaction was to ask, "How can you talk about AIDS and be cheerful?" At the time, Gary had been gone only six months. If there is anything about the experience to be grateful for, it is that I was alone with him when he died. I was with him when he came into the world, and I wanted to be with him when he left it.

I had just met Jon, a new young friend, to whom I expressed my dilemma about the assigned topic. He replied, "That's how to start your presentation. That it is difficult to not be sad. But tell them how good your life has been in the last few months." Of course, he was taking some of the credit for my newfound attitude, and I must admit that he provided many opportunities to be cheerful. His presence in my life helped me find the balance and strength I needed to attend funerals, memorial services, candlelight vigils and marches, or sometimes just a peaceful bedside visit. So I told the audience that, during my twelve-year involvement with people with AIDS through AIDS Foundation Houston, the AIDS support group of which I was a member, and the individuals who came into—and went out of—my life, my grief was immense and nearly overwhelming; but my life was better for having been a participant in the trenches and in the quiet background.

For most of my life, up to 1983, I had searched for a cause; a means of contributing to the betterment of society, or even a small part of it that needed help. I served on committees and walked in the March of Dimes Mothers March, and spent countless hours as a VA hospital volunteer, but I didn't have the urgency of involvement that motivates those who have personal reasons for springing into action.

In 1983, my action became a compulsion and I jumped into the fray. I say "the fray" because that is what it was at the time. The participants included the government, homophobes, the medical establishment, the media, employers, landlords, and even many funeral homes, which would not handle the bodies of those infected with the deadly virus. It was not unusual for some people diagnosed with AIDS to be disowned by their family. One young man's father received a call from a volunteer attorney, who informed him of his son's death. When asked what he wanted his son's caregivers to do with the body, the father replied, "Put it in a garbage bag and put it out by the curb."

Even though I was devastated by what was happening—history in the making—I thought I was giving of myself. And the most wonderful thing happened to me. I was getting what I felt I had been missing for so much of my life: appreciation, attention, recognition, social activity, and above all, love!

My greatest reward came from the pride my son had for what I was doing. He shared it with his friends and doctors. He asked me to help the mothers of his dying friends in San Francisco. During one of my visits with him, there was a grieving mother who had come from across the country to tearfully wait a week or so, until she could take her only child, Allen, back to Tennessee—in "cargo hold," as she put it. Together, Gary and I tried to comfort her. The next day, Allen died and was on his way to eternity via Memphis.

My original motive had been to prepare myself for the possibility of my son dying before I did. It was awkward, though, to talk to him about treatments that I had heard of, in order to see if he could try them, because he was determined to live his life without having it controlled by this new interloper. I wanted to inform him of the deaths of another, and yet another, of my own assigned charges, but I realized that wasn't going to help *him* at all. There were some things I just couldn't share with him. For example, when the second person I helped died two months after I had met him, I called Gary. He could tell by my voice that my new friend was gone. I knew right then that I was not going to keep him apprised of the setbacks or losses I was dealing with, because it pulled him down. He was bent on maintaining his positive attitude, and I had to learn to be selective about the information I passed along to him. I knew he was deeply concerned for me and his empathy was sincere, but my realization that I was telling him what might lay ahead on his own journey clarified for me that sharing such information was sorely inappropriate.

As time went on, the researchers continued to extend their estimate of the time it would take for answers, treatment, or maybe even a cure, always in five-year increments.

My son, in his short life, continually sought spiritual fulfillment. He joined various groups in search of truth and enlightenment. Becoming a Rosicrucian fulfilled that need for him until he began to study with the Sufi Order in San Francisco.

This last avenue, where he claimed to have reached that enlightenment, was begun by Mevlana Jelaluddin Rumi. After Rumi's death, his followers founded the Mevlevi Order, also known as the "Whirling Dervishes," who created the *sema*, their sacred turning dance ceremony. Before beginning, they ask permission to begin turning by kissing the sheikh's hand, and the dervish's sikke (a tall fez hat which must be earned at a particular stage of Sufi learning) is kissed by the sheikh in affirmation. Rumi wrote thousands of poems about love. One Sufi verse says, "When the heart weeps for what it's lost, the soul rejoices for what it's found." The answer to the original question of how my life has been changed by AIDS is, *my soul is rejoicing!*

For Gary

1.

Before and After

The snow at Crater Lake was fourteen feet deep, or did the ranger say forty-eight feet, that December in 1982? He said we were standing that high above a dozen picnic tables, buried in a record snowfall for the area. If we hadn't had snowshoes, we might have walked right over the edge of the crater. The snow had built up to about ten feet beyond the rim, and one misstep would have put us into the canyon far below.

It was the second big vacation we had had together since Gary moved to California. The first one, the year before, had been to Yosemite, where we had Christmas dinner on a gigantic fallen redwood tree. This year, it was in the middle of a snowplowed road in Oregon. We could set our picnic meal anywhere we wanted; there would be no traffic coming through. During the snowshoe hike, he dropped a mitten at the top of a hill. It tumbled end over end, and he chased it all the way down, until he was running faster than his snowshoes would let him. And there he was, mitten in hand, sitting in the snow at the bottom of the hill, rolling with laughter, as the rest of the snowshoed group above joined in.

That is my last image of Gary before the diagnosis. A few weeks later, he called to inform me of a swollen lymph node on his neck. His barber, having noticed it, suggested a visit to the doctor. Apparently, the barber was more aware of what was soon to become an all too common event in the gay community. Five months earlier, Gary had sent me a reprint of an article from a medical journal, describing the sudden appearance of a rare cancer that seemed to be affecting only gay men. What was happening? Who knew what was to come?

"Nothing to worry about," Gary had written, "just for your information."

A biopsy was to be scheduled, but because of a previously planned ski trip, it was postponed. The doctor had said there was no urgency. That seemed odd at the time, but in retrospect we learned it was indeed true. Kaposi's sarcoma (KS) was the least of concerns when he could have been diagnosed with other life-threatening infections. Within a few weeks, the "nothing to worry about" became very worrisome. That rare cancer was in the lymph node. And so it began. Staging, they called it then. A series of blood tests, antigen tests, various "-scopies." And then wait.

Gary asked his primary care doctor how many patients he had with the new illness. The reply was, "Four."

"And where are they now?" Gary questioned him.

"One died, one is doing fine, one is sick, and the fourth committed suicide. Don't do anything rash."

Friends called him, mostly out of curiosity, but the attention Gary wanted most was for someone to just ask, "How about going out for a pizza?"

The day he called to tell me of his diagnosis, we were both at work. He was a computer specialist working as a technical associate of the Particle Data Group at Lawrence Berkeley Laboratory at the University of California, Berkeley. One of the major publications in which he participated was *Physics Letters B*, a journal devoted to the rapid publication of important new results in nuclear and particle physics. Gary and an associate also prepared an annual Pocket Diary for Physicists, which was distributed worldwide. Both of them were acknowledged in the publications, along with the scientific team.

I was the office manager for a store-planning firm, which provided floor plans, merchandising, and décor for retail establishments; mostly large department stores. Throughout the day, I called Gary to ask how he was taking the news, how he was feeling, how he could work after getting the diagnosis. His answer was, "If people would stop calling me so much, I would be doing much better."

Therefore, it was up to me to deal with my own anxiety. I panicked, I cried, I worried. What was a mother to do? I expected the worst, and didn't know how to convey my concern without Gary feeling that I was nagging or leaning on him. Initially, I couldn't think logically enough to figure out that a weekly call would be fine. And instead of asking how he was feeling, I would ask, "What are you doing?" The first time I tried that approach and he told me he was hanging track lights in his thirty-foot hallway, I realized it would be exactly the system I should use from then on. If he was well enough to do such strenuous tasks, then he must be feeling all right. He didn't want anyone persisting in asking about his health. He worked at his regular job at the lab, and he forged ahead with his home remodeling, deliberately insisting that his diagnosis was not going to take control of his life. He was determined to deal with it as it came, and not put it before the stuff of life that gave him joy and fulfillment.

My niece, Nancy, was graduating from college in San Jose in May, and that became a good reason for a trip to San Francisco. I was so relieved to see Gary in such good health and high spirits that it was difficult to realize the enormity of what was happening. He was very protective of me with regard to sharing food from his plate, making sure that my fork didn't touch any part of what had been touched by his. We soon learned that the virus could not be passed along that way, but his concern was ever present.

On May 1, 1983, we went to the home of Mark, a new friend of Gary's, whose mother had come from New York to be with her son. It was the first of many times that I would see a hospital bed set up in someone's living room. Mark was too weak to eat dinner, but his mother insisted that Gary and I join her in the kitchen, and we talked about what the future seemed to hold for the gay population.

The next morning, Gary invited me to go with him to an appointment at San Francisco General Hospital initiated by his primary care doctor. Until that morning, I wasn't aware that he had an appointment, so I was quite nervous about it. In the car, he said, "While I'm at it, I think I'll ask the doctor about the thing on my leg."

More gulping and shaking on my part.

"What thing on your leg?"

We arrived early, in the darkness of what would become a gray day in San Francisco, before the hospital staff's day shift made an appearance. The lights in the building had not yet been turned on, adding to the dreary ambiance. I didn't realize how shaken Gary was until the first arrival on duty prepared a "permanent" plastic identification card for him, and he was told, "Just present this card every time you come here and it will speed the process along."

Every time you come here? What was Gary in for?

Then they gave him a legal-sized document to read and

sign. His hands were trembling as he read it, and as I tried to read it with him, my head was swimming with fear.

When the young Dr. Paul Volberding invited us into his examination room, Gary was prepared with his yellow pad to take notes, but he asked to borrow my pen. That was something of a giveaway as to his mental state. He was usually so very organized that he would have brought his own. It was a rather uneventful visit, but highly marked by the fact that it was the first of many more doctor visits and of Gary's fears of his own role in this new phase of his life. Never having been ill before was one wonderful thing; even if he had been, a healthy immune system would have worked its magic to take him through the course of an ordinary illness. But this illness was one which slowly destroyed the immune system. How could he know when, or how, this unexpected behemoth would force itself into his everyday life?

As it turned out, that day Dr. Volberding had just wanted to perform a routine checkup of his patients (who, at the time, were few). But while we were there, Gary took the opportunity to ask about the small lesion on his leg. The doctor told him they needed to do a biopsy, and it would take a week to get the results from the lab. Since Gary had to take a business trip to New Orleans, he received the news while he was away from home—that the biopsy showed nothing.

After Gary buttoned his shirt to leave Dr. Volberding's office at San Francisco General Hospital that cold, dreary day, he forgot to tuck it into his pants. He also left my pen on the table. Both were small incidents, but very telling of his fear. My heart broke for him.

As we left Dr. Volberding's office, I said to him, "Please take care of my son."

And he replied, "We will."

At the time, I assumed the doctor was much older than Gary and had the experience to meet the crisis, but later learned that he was then only thirty-three years old. For three years prior to his assignment, in 1981, as Chief of Oncology at San Francisco General Hospital, he had been researching retroviruses. On the first day at his new job, he was introduced to a patient with Kaposi's sarcoma, the same rare cancer of connective tissue written about in the medical journal article Gary had sent me six months earlier. There was some measure of reassurance in knowing that, for two years, he had been familiar with what Gary had been diagnosed. But he was not to be Gary's doctor for very long. He soon left his position after receiving notification of a grant for AIDS research, for which he was appointed principal investigator. So things were looking up. Or so we thought. The gay community, in general, stood to benefit, as we assumed new research would quickly have the problem solved. Gary and everyone else who was infected, but still alive, could go back to the life they knew before AIDS ever came on the scene.

Later that same day—May 2, 1983—after our visit to San Francisco General, we gathered at Castro and Market Streets to participate in the candlelight march to the United Nations Plaza, in the company of what was later estimated to be six thousand people, whose concern surely matched ours. Mark and a dozen others led the march, carrying a banner which read "Fighting for Our Lives." Some who could barely walk, and some who didn't walk at all, spoke to the assembled throng. I don't know how Mark mustered the strength to show up, considering how sick he had been the day before, when he was confined to bed during our visit with him and his mother. As we sang "Amazing Grace," Gary wrapped his arms around my waist and held me close. To this day, I cannot hear that song without remembering the emotion-packed night in San Francisco, when AIDS was all so new and we were all so desperate. We cried as we sang, and throughout the event, the Sisters of Perpetual Indulgence—who, according to their Internet website, claim to have orchestrated the vigil—took up a collection. (I have read of others' claims of organizing the candlelight march.) The Sisters is a 501(c)(3) nonprofit order, founded in 1979, of "nuns" (female and male, but not to be confused with Catholic nuns) who believe in the promulgation of universal joy and the expiation of stigmatic guilt. Their mission is "to ruin all detrimental conditions, including complacency, guilt and the inability to laugh at one's self." While they evoke humor in their dress, behavior, and the individual names they adopt for themselves, such as Sister Roxanne Roles, they are about community involvement and fund-raising for a variety of worthy causes to expand their ministry and education.

The speakers at the gathering encouraged us to call the White House the next day and demand action from the government. When I called the next morning, I asked the operator if they were receiving many calls. I wasn't sure what "many" meant, but he assured me that they were. Maybe this thing wasn't going to be a crisis after all, not if we had anything to do with it. The medical community didn't seem to have solutions; it was too new to them. There was no history to fall back on.

Knowing that the disease was incurable caused me to realize that if I saw my son only once a year, even if he lived another twenty years, I would only see him twenty times— less than most people with healthy relationships see their loved ones in a month, if they reside in the same area. Yet, Gary insisted on living his life as he had before the diagnosis, and I had to honor his decision.

As Dr. Volberding became more and more involved in research, Gary's new primary physician took the approach of "relying on the patient's condition rather than the [lab] numbers." Thankfully, that would work for Gary for the next ten years, but surely, a cure was just around the corner.

1983

2.
Getting Started

Returning home to Texas from the highly charged events out west, I called Gary's doctor in San Francisco for suggestions of how to get involved, both for Gary and myself. I had to meet the enemy head-on in order to prepare myself for what was to come. Among the groups he suggested I call were the gay hotline and the gay counseling center. By the next morning, I was speaking with a young man who conducted an AIDS support group. It turned out that he was a therapist, who would soon become *my* therapist. I had, in the meantime, hurried to a recommended psychiatrist, who spent three hours talking with me about how I'd better rush out to California to be with my son, who "would be dead in a year." The next day, I met with the therapist for what I thought was to be a discussion of the crisis. He said I had to decide whether I was going to continue seeing him, or the three-hour doctor. Now I was getting somewhere. Needless to say, I chose him. Besides, his name was Gary, and I liked that. To get me started on involvement, he referred me to a young woman who was attempting to set up an office for an AIDS Foundation. She had forms being used by the New York Gay Men's Health Crisis, but needed similar ones for the Houston group. She was a medical student, a dancer, and a cocktail waitress, but she was not a typist. And typing was what she needed, so she needed me. All I had to do to get started that afternoon was to create client and volunteer intake forms, confidentiality statements, and a few other assorted necessities of the new, all-volunteer organization, make fifty copies of each, and deliver them to her apartment by 6:00 that evening before her dinner guests arrived. Having met the challenge, I was in—as if any even mildly interested individual would have been turned away.

1983

3.
In the Beginning

With no experience in serving the needs of those who were becoming ill with this new disease, five or six people met one Saturday in June 1983, one month after I returned from San Francisco, to participate in a weekend training session for new volunteers of the KS/AIDS Foundation. Originally, the Foundation was called the KS Committee, because at the time, Kaposi's sarcoma had become the first common diagnosis among the newly infected. As other infections became associated with Acquired Immune Deficiency Syndrome, it was renamed KS/AIDS Foundation, and became a 501(c)(3) organization. Ultimately, with so many other AIDS-related infections being diagnosed, the name was soon changed to AIDS Foundation Houston (AFH).

Prior to our weekend training session, there were a few people who had realized the necessity of mobilizing troops to face this enemy charging head-on into our lives. The Montrose Counseling Center, primarily serving gays and lesbians, had already been established as a safe place where people felt comfortable coming out of the closet. When the new illness arrived, a small group of the center's therapists, including my therapist, became part of a team which created the KS Committee and the volunteer training program.

The evolution of the foundation began with a single individual, Michael McAdory, the manager of a popular gay bar, who became ill and went to his doctor to be treated. With no successful diagnosis or treatment there, he went to MD Anderson, a world-renowned cancer treatment hospital in Houston. Fortunately, his doctor there, Peter Mansell, was a researcher who had heard through the grapevine that people in Los Angeles and New York were going to their doctors with KS and pneumocystis carnii pneumonia (PCP). He was curious about what this new phenomenon was, and the common denominator that linked its sufferers. He learned that the common denominator was that they were all gay men. Dr. Mansell became very intrigued, as did Robert Awe, the physician at the local county hospital, who was then seeing many uninsured patients with illnesses the hospital had never before treated.

As if being uninsured weren't a burden in itself, medical insurance companies were screening applicants by marital status, ZIP codes, and any other criteria they could use to disqualify gay men for coverage. So, if a person was a single male living in the Montrose area of Houston, he was denied medical insurance because of the company's biased assumption that he might have AIDS. He would then be referred by his doctor to the county hospital. Of course, those with in-force insurance policies were welcomed at the other hospitals, where the doctors were knowledgeable and had figured out that AIDS was an expensive disease. If insurance was going to pay for treatment, they were more than willing to accept those patients. There would be no cure; treatment of the particular illness for which the person was admitted and maintenance of the patient's health were all they could provide.

Meanwhile, nobody else was doing anything about the problem in Houston. The interest in it began when Michael McAdory, who was known by many people in the community from the bar he managed, chose to come out and start talking to his friends. Finally, receiving the diagnosis of Kaposi's sarcoma, he pushed people to do research and education, and urged the gay community to respond. Along with the therapists at the counseling center, Michael, Sue Lovell, and a few others formed the KS Committee. At that time, there were doctors who wouldn't see any of these patients because everybody was panic-stricken. They didn't know how the disease was spread; they thought it was contagious. They knew nothing. In addition to the physicians who were refusing to see people with KS or PCP, no hospitals would admit them either—or they were isolating them in quarantine. People were fighting because there was no information. Houston's large medical center, including MD Anderson, was urged to become active, and they responded by admitting the first AIDS patients in Houston.

Yet it was still not known how the disease was spread. By then, there was fear everywhere, but in the gay community, there was a lot of fear. That is how the counseling center got pulled in, because people were going to their therapists and saying, "I'm concerned, I don't know if I have this disease, I'm scared, I don't know if I'm I going to die. What do I do?" And those therapists were the people who were trying to deal with it on a therapeutic basis. They became involved because they had to be able to communicate with their clients, who were fearful because of what was happening in their community.

The Montrose Clinic, with clients in the gay community, began doing a great deal of testing, so it became inevitable that those three organizations—the KS Committee, the Montrose Counseling Center, and the Montrose Clinic—the string of pearls, as Sue Lovell referred to them, had to work together very closely.

During this time, another Michael, who worked for MD

Anderson as a medical journalist, wrote articles on research being done there, putting out information about the hospital and many of its educational pamphlets. Thus, working very closely with Dr. Mansell, the KS Committee, including the journalist, Michael Wilson (who would later become the KS/AIDS Foundation's second president; Michael McAdory having been the first), was able to use whatever information they had gathered about the new illness, which was ultimately discovered to be sexually transmitted. Yet nobody was making that information public. In time, it would be learned that transmission was also possible from blood transfusions, the sharing of needles for intravenous drug use, and from a pregnant HIV-positive woman to her unborn child.

There was talk of quarantining *gay* people. The medical response had always been to quarantine people during epidemics. How else could they keep it from spreading? But with this, it couldn't be done because they realized it was so widespread, and its discovery was years after people had been exposed and their symptoms were just beginning to appear. Some people were saying, "Don't get tested" because they were afraid of being "outed," as there was no guarantee of confidentiality.

A group called Citizens for Human Equality gave the KS Committee $5,000 to write and distribute a brochure using information from Dr. Mansell, saying the infection was sexually transmitted. He told the group that it was their responsibility to tell the Houston gay community how the disease was spread and to educate them about how to take care of themselves, stressing not to be afraid. In addition to the committee receiving a great deal of criticism, the Houston public health department denied it was a problem. They didn't want to touch it because doing so would have required talking about sex and condoms;

there was no way they were going to consider it. Since the City of Houston Health Department denied there were any cases of PCP or KS, they were not doing any epidemiology or requiring doctors to report to them.

The committee conducted a survey in the gay community to find out which doctors the men were using. Some were gay-friendly; so naturally, the men would go to them. The doctors allowed the committee to go through their files to determine the illnesses they were treating. Other doctors were asked for the same privilege, that of looking for patients who had PCP, KS, thrush, or other symptoms. The result of the search was that almost every doctor's records showed that they had hundreds of cases. The committee then reached out to other doctors at MD Anderson who knew of people who were being treated with still other symptoms.

After gathering the statistics, the KS Committee took them to the mayor, compelling the city council to require tracking such incidences of similar illnesses. The city council, though reluctant, then required the City of Houston Health Department to begin doing epidemiology and reporting, so the KS Committee could gather even more statistics to see how widespread it was and the significance of that—other than that it was good public health policy. Although funding was becoming available, Houston hadn't been able to get any of it because the city hadn't been able to show the need, simply because the health department had not been maintaining statistics. The funding was going only to areas where they felt that the foundations were working in cooperation with their city and county health departments. Needless to say, Houston lost out on a number of large initial grants because of that.

All of this activity was taking place during the time when the gay community in Houston was enjoying the passage by the city council of an ordinance to protect gay and lesbian city employees from being fired. The ordinance passed ten to five, but the community lost its nondiscrimination status by four to one in a referendum vote. There were political people who had been allies of the gay and lesbian community, but they were upset with the mayor at the time for other reasons, so there were many different issues that factored into the referendum. This was another reason Houston didn't receive the funds it needed, because they were caught up in the referendum. There was a huge backlash on the gay community because of the issue of nondiscrimination in the City of Houston workplace. None of the politicians and policy makers would do anything about AIDS because they were afraid there would be a powerful body of people that would take them to task for helping out, since AIDS was seen strictly as a gay issue. The elected city officials felt that the gay community was too toxic and they couldn't have anything to do with them. In turn, the city health department wouldn't do anything to help distribute information. The next year, no elected officials would choose to be endorsed by the gay political caucus.

Partnering the city's political troubles with the gay community, and then with KS, there was a tremendous amount of fear and misinformation. In that climate, there was still no assistance, as there was in other states such as California and New York. By then, some of the other major cities had received grant money that was becoming available, such as the Robert Wood Johnson Grant. The Centers for Disease Control was also starting to put out grant money, but Houston received none of it because of its inability to show evidence of the need. The health departments in the other city, county, and state governments pitched in and helped because they realized that there was an epidemic which was a public health issue, and they needed to be involved with it.

The Houston KS Committee raised money to get educational information out to the community and, together with medical people, created a safe sex program. None of these activities were funded by grants of any kind, but rather by the KS Committee—which, in its earliest days, had raised money to go to MD Anderson Hospital and ask them to do the study.

A lot was happening around the country in the first five years, but Houston's AIDS groups were *still* unable to get grant money—even though they had printed the first ever AIDS booklet, designed and held the first safe-sex program, and went out and taught it to other AIDS foundations around the United States because it was so effective. The other cities went to their state governments and received grant funding to promote the program while we were still having fund-raisers, such as walkathons, bartenders giving their tips, and anything else to raise money. Houston was the fourth-largest city in the country with the fourth-largest number of people who were affected. We started it all, but the other three cities were getting the funding grants. Their city and county governments had recognized that it was an emergency and that it was important.

The KS Committee used any method they could think of to get the word out. Special calendars were printed and sold. Flyers were distributed outside of gay bars, where the management also allowed the handing out of condoms. Fund-raisers were held at bars where the managers agreed to turn off the dance music for a while so the bar patrons could be told what they needed to know.

Parties were planned where people could invite their

friends and there would be a safe-sex presentation about how they could protect themselves. The KS Committee recruited attractive men from the gay community to go out to the bars, where they were allowed to get the attention of the patrons to advertise that there would be safe-sex workshops at the clinic and the counseling center. Another means of educating the at-risk population was by having these men wear Levi's 501 blue jeans, with a specially designed, three-fold-panel brochure which fit into the back pocket where it would be seen. It was easy to distribute the brochures because of their high visibility. These men circulated at the gay bars and took advantage of every opportunity they could to get the word out.

Some people on the committee were reluctant to show any visual representation of sexual activity, including stick figures or drawings of any kind, until research had shown that stuffed animals could be used to discuss the controversial issue of safe sex practices. By using actual stuffed animals, particularly teddy bears, or drawings of them, it was easier for people to accept the images being depicted in the safe-sex presentations

When the Houston KS Committee put out the booklet, some groups across the nation were very upset with them, believing it would set back gay rights. There were still other groups that applauded them and said, "Good for you. You have the integrity to stand up and say what is really happening." It was a time when gays were just beginning to get some long sought after rights in this country, and there was fear that the AIDS issue was being used to take away at least a few of those newly won rights. But the main focus was to get as many of the booklets as possible out to people so they would be informed, and so that information could start to allay some of the fear— by clarifying, for instance, that the disease was not transmitted because someone coughed, or because they shook hands. A lot of the fear could be put to rest, but the gay community needed to set about stopping its spread.

Of course, they knew they could not stop people from having sex. That wasn't going to happen. They were determined to enlighten them about methods of doing so safely. People needed to know what kinds of sexual acts were most conducive to passing along the mysterious illness. That is when the issue of condoms came up, and a safe-sex campaign was created to educate people on their use. The committee met with medical people and others who knew how to present the information. It was promoted as an educational program, but really it was a PR campaign. What had originally been called "safe sex" was later changed to "safer sex," because people had to understand that some of the methods of reducing risk were not always fail-safe.

Besides MD Anderson, the county hospital, and the hospitals which accepted the insured, a new hospital was opened which would treat only people with AIDS. There was a great deal of opposition to that hospital because of the stigma, reminding people of the days of TB clinics in hospitals. It was soon realized that if this facility existed, no other hospital would accept these patients. They would be told, "Go to that hospital." But very soon, there was no longer the capacity to handle the growing number of patients, and it became important to inform other hospitals that it was safe to take people with AIDS. Once there was more information about it, people had the right to go to the hospital of their choice.

There was the issue that the bathhouses ought to be closed down, but doing so wouldn't stop certain behavior. It would only drive people underground. The campaign provided a great educational tool for speakers who went to the bathhouses to teach the men about practicing safe sex, and what would happen if they didn't. It was worse than playing Russian roulette. The behavior wouldn't stop, but the educational information had to be disseminated nevertheless.

By the time of the next Annual International Gay and Lesbian Health Conference, AIDS was included. The following year, the subject of AIDS was treated separately from other health matters, but the two conferences were held at the same time because there were people there for health issues who were not really involved with HIV/AIDS. The People with AIDS Coalition (PWAC) was formed at those conferences. PWA's came out with their own Bill of Rights, stating how they expected to be treated, not only by the medical community and their own government, but by their own community. Their statement went to the federal government, the Centers for Disease Control (CDC), and the National Institutes of Health (NIH), telling them what was expected.

When it was figured out how the virus was transmitted, which by then included receiving infected blood and blood products through transfusions, the blood banks had to know how to protect the blood supply. Questions arose, such as: How far has this been spread through the population, and what are the needs going to be? And mainly, how could it be stopped? All the while, they were trying to come out with any sort of medication, initially AZT. But the main concern was how to stop it from spreading.

The blood banks had a routine questionnaire which donors were asked to complete before their blood was drawn. One of the questions asked if the donor was in a high-risk group; which, of course, was threatening to gay men. At worst, they might not be truthful in their response, and that was not a viable option. During that time, people weren't coming out—if they did, they risked not only discrimination because of their sexual orientation, but the assumption that they were also HIV-positive.

Finally, the blood banks used a bar code system and everyone could donate without giving their name. The bar-coded questionnaires were completed and turned in with the matching bar-coded bag of blood. Everybody trusted that by law, the blood banks had to abide by the rules of confidentiality. If the question had been answered affirmatively—that one was in a high-risk group, or had been exposed to the virus—then immediately that bag of blood would be discarded. At least that method allowed gay individuals to stay in the closet, but still protected the blood supply.

As more and more people required more and more social services, the KS/AIDS Foundation became a multipurpose foundation. In addition to assisting people with housing costs, financial help, and legal needs, the foundation provided rooms at McAdory House. This was a ninety-day, interim living facility named for Michael McAdory, where people awaiting their first Social Security payment could reside until they had the means to afford rent elsewhere. The residents had to be ambulatory and able to care for themselves, as the home was not an assisted living facility, but was an important service for those in need of temporary shelter.

McAdory House was the first of its kind in the country, as was Stone Soup, the first AIDS food pantry—which, at its inception, was located in McAdory House. The foundation eventually bought other apartment buildings and offered rental assistance for permanent housing specifically for people living with AIDS. In addition to these many services, the AIDS Foundation became a source of referrals to other agencies.

4.

Basic Training

The first day of our AIDS Foundation volunteer training session, we were taught that we were not to refer to those infected as patients, but as clients. We were to understand that no matter how much we became a part of their lives and their care, or how close we became to them as friends, if family members intervened and wanted matters handled differently from what we were doing, we were to defer to them.

We learned the importance of bleach and latex gloves, which later became something of a nonissue in carrying out everyday routine chores. It was confusing as to whether we were safeguarding the client from harmful germs because of their impaired immune system, or if it was our own health we were protecting by not touching anything they had touched. Paranoia abounded, but only in proportion to the lack of knowledge about the disease. We talked about how we could help those affected, with no one—particularly the medical community—knowing that a virus was the cause of the illness.

It appeared to me that all of the other new volunteers were gay men. When asked their reason for coming forward to join the meager number of people who wanted to do something about the onrushing crisis, they all told of a friend, lover, family member, acquaintance, or someone other than themselves who had been diagnosed or had died from an illness or infection which would later be attributed to HIV. Or perhaps, they were infected and wanted to be on what was then the front line of information. At that time, mid-1983, the cause of the illness was being studied, but no official announcement had yet been made.

I was quite at ease within the gay community; in fact, it was my primary comfort zone. My son, Gary, had seen to that. Over the years, he had introduced me to his friends, lovers, and the Gay Men's Chorus of San Francisco. During my annual holiday visits, he was usually invited to friends' homes for Christmas dinner, and there was no question that I was also invited. I loved being with him, his friends, and any other gay people who came into my life. They welcomed me with open arms and I was happy to fill them. That feeling extended to gay people, especially men, wherever I was. So as I sat with my new friends at the training session, I had no misgivings about my decision to participate. In those early days, although there were other women volunteering for other assignments, I believe I was the singular parent in this all-volunteer army.

Each training participant received a little teddy bear as a thank-you gift and memento. Without peeking, each person drew out their own bear from a large paper grocery sack, and I couldn't help but notice that I was the one who received the only white bear—the significance being that I wanted the white one. It was good karma for me. Because of its role in teaching safe-sex practices, the teddy bear had become a symbol of the AIDS educational program.

We did some role-playing exercises to prepare us mentally and emotionally for handling whatever might come our way. No one in attendance had known each other before, and though I was somewhat apprehensive, that soon dissipated as I realized that we were all in it together and had to forge ahead if we were going to prevail. In one exercise, we were paired off and instructed to stare into each other's eyes for three minutes without speaking. It became very intense for my partner, David, and me, as those three minutes became an eternity. I, choking back tears, could no longer contain myself. David sensed the overwhelming emotion, and there we were, both with tears streaming down our faces. It provided a very profound, spiritual bonding, which we had questioned at the beginning, but silently understood by the time it was over. Learning to sense another's pain or emotional level without the benefit of conversation was to become an intense and valuable asset when we were faced with similar events during the care of the people we would soon be meeting. It was likely that they might be attached to a breathing ventilator, or perhaps might have dementia. Sometimes, they might be too weak to communicate, but would know the value of a silent visitor who gave reassurance by simply being with them.

We took turns acting out scenes of hospital or home visits where the volunteer and the ill person had never before met each other. Ad-libbing conversations in such dire circumstances was much too difficult to carry out with ease. The only consolation I felt about fumbling through it was that everyone there shared the same apprehension. We did the best we could and were not chastised for our lack of savoir faire, nor were we criticized for our poor acting ability. In truth, it was easier to use these skills in real-life settings. The words came naturally—sometimes effectively, and sometimes not—but I believe that the recipients accepted that we were trying our very best to comfort them.

Many of the volunteers felt a sense of guilt if we took time out for social events, such as dinners together, movies, or parties. We were healthy; we were supposed to be taking care of the sick and dying. Ted, the head of the Social Services Committee, who conducted the weekly volunteer meetings, reassured us that we must not take on that guilt for indulging in normal activities. His profound statement left a permanent impression.

"If you spread yourself too thin, you won't be any good to anybody."

Ted was a therapist. He knew the right things to say.

In those early days, our weekly volunteer meetings consisted of eight to ten people sitting on the floor of a donated empty room of a bank building. We exchanged what little information we had to relate to the others who had taken the plunge. An AIDS hotline phone number had been established, to respond to callers who wanted confidential answers to confidential questions. One of the assignments of the person on duty at the one-man phone bank was to log the incoming calls in a dated journal, with a brief description of the call. This helped us to gather data about the many different aspects of how the illness was affecting people. I was very apprehensive about volunteering for hotline duty, mostly from a fear of not having a ready answer for people who might be calling in a panicked state, which I felt inadequately prepared to handle.

A young gay man, braver than I, reported a memorable story. He had received a call one evening from a frantic office manager. The caller said, "We just found out that one of our employees is gay! What should we do with all of the files in the office?"

The volunteer laughingly told our group, "I was very tempted to tell her to burn them all."

1983

5.

Regrouping

After winging it for six months, but with a semblance of order and an immense will to serve the fast-growing number of clients, it became necessary to provide more training for the volunteers. After all, even the therapists and board members who had organized the foundation were developing the strategies for dealing with the clients' needs based on input from the volunteers. In fact, it was mandatory that we receive more training so that we would uniformly represent the foundation. I was continually eager to gain new information which would bolster my self-confidence. I knew we were performing valuable tasks, and my mission continued to provide me with satisfaction and a profound sense of pride.

December 11 brought together a new group of volunteer trainees—*all six* of us: Ken, Buddy, Cecil, Chris, Steve, and me.

Ken sold women's shoes at one of the country's leading fashion stores, this one catering to the elite of Houston society. He was no ordinary "shoe dog." He interacted with his regular clients, phoning them when a style perfectly suited for them arrived. He most likely was involved in ordering merchandise that would, without question, be bought without even having to be previewed by these ladies, who were too busy preparing for and attending the various charity events that usually rated mention in the newspapers' society columns. He helped the managers of the other fashion departments in the store coordinate complete outfits for out-of-town clients who maintained homes in multiple cities, having lunch served to them in the store's commodious dressing rooms. They would make their annual or semiannual visits to their favorite fashion mecca to shop for the latest goodies with which to stock their multiple closets. Ken lovingly referred to one customer from Illinois as Our Lady of Chicago, and visions of commissions danced in his twinkling eyes when he spoke of her. There was no doubt about it, Ken was charming, and it was difficult to remember that his financial station was more in line with ours than with the clients he indulged.

It did not surprise me to learn that Ken had been married (with children) before coming out, but only after his children were grown. He was a ladies' man in addition to being a man's man. By the time AIDS came into his life, he had the edge of maturity over many of the younger gay men who hadn't begun to grapple with its enormity, never mind its very existence.

Ken and I usually had dinner together on Friday nights after work. One restaurant in the predominantly gay neighborhood became our ritual hangout. We frequented the place so much that, after many months of ordering the same thing every week, I began to request a change of scenery. But Ken, not one to forfeit a chance to mingle with the familiar crowd, ignored my wishes. I teased him about his car being set on automatic pilot when we left his house for dinner. He not only didn't think my jabs were humorous, he totally ignored them. And as much as cigarette smoke annoyed me and my nasal passages, he would insist that we sit in the smoking section. One time, when the only available table was in nonsmoking, I expressed my delight that we would be able to sit where I wanted to, for a change. But he declared, "We'll wait!"

It was clear to me that if I was going to travel in his circle, in order to get more involved with the AIDS community and to be his friend, I was going to have to buy that relationship with submissiveness. We had many meals together, saw stage plays, went to operas and movies, and attended parties. Before we left the house to see the movie *Terms of Endearment,* Ken advised me to take a box of tissues with me because he knew it would be a real tearjerker. I was still waiting for an occasion to open the package when I stole a glance to my left to see how Ken was holding up. He was sound asleep.

Over the following years, we became even closer allies and our work with the AIDS Foundation grew, causing our social life to expand along with the work. One of the gatherings we attended in 1988 was a reception for Randy Shilts, author of *And the Band Played On.* Shilts was not only very informative about his source of information for the book, as medical reporter for the *San Francisco Chronicle,* but he regaled us with personal stories of his travels around the country, bearing urgent messages relating to what would be coming down the pike with regard to AIDS. Although some of the experiences he told us about were incredibly humorous, we had to remind ourselves that they were at the expense of the issue of AIDS. He cheerfully signed our copies of his book, along with an encouraging message on the face page. Mine read, "To Freda, thanks for your work. Keep caring. October 2, 1988. Randy Shilts"

I found it ironic that the date of the book signing was the third anniversary of the reference in the opening line of his book. He wrote that by October 2, 1985, the day Rock Hudson died, AIDS was a familiar word to almost every household in the Western world.

But four years before we met Randy Shilts, Ken and I

were still getting to know each other. The parties we attended together were usually AIDS-related and there were many, but if there were any other segments of the population whose company Ken enjoyed, I was not his date. He knew other people who were not affiliated with the AIDS Foundation and somehow he made time for them, in addition to his demanding job of making certain that his society customers were well shod. That was all right with me; I was trying to keep my own life in a separate compartment, which often was difficult to do.

Buddy was a handsome man in his mid-thirties and was very attentive to me. We had many good times together. Going out to dinner with him was more adventurous than it was with Ken because we went to a variety of restaurants. At a very popular pizza parlor, I remember waiting an interminably long time for our pizza to arrive—only to realize that we had filled up on breadsticks and wine during the wait. The pizza was great, though, even if we did have to take it home with us and wait until the next day to find out. Buddy was eager to help with team assignments; however, he was in the throes of a lost love relationship and was not the least bit shy about confiding in me about it. It was, I think, the first time in my life that I realized that when a person complains incessantly about how badly they were treated by their former lover, they are really saying how desperately they still love them. Poor Buddy was in this condition when we met. He worked for a large firm which manufactured fasteners, and he had a thorough knowledge of every nut, bolt, screw, and rivet in the plant. He was good at his job, but in his private life, he was miserable.

Cecil was a nurse at the Veterans Administration Hospital. We were fortunate to have him on our team, with his working knowledge of the medical field, even though the new field of AIDS had barely begun to surface. He apparently dropped out as a volunteer after working with our first client; perhaps it was too overwhelming for him, or maybe he became too busy with his full-time nursing job as AIDS worked its way into the VA Hospital. He may have notified the AIDS Foundation, but I never saw him again.

Chris pretty much disappeared from our little group before he had put in an appearance at anyone's bedside, as far as our team knew. I never saw him after our training session. Perhaps he was frightened of what he might have to face. Maybe he, himself, was sick. At that time, many people wanted to help but couldn't muster the courage. Who knows what motivates the doers? This is not to say that I wasn't scared as hell or that I looked forward to facing the inevitable epidemic. I simply had a fierce drive to do something for my son's benefit. Chris had his own reasons for not returning to our group. He may have joined another crusade. We should have checked on him—not for ourselves, but to be sure he was okay. It was often difficult to decide whether to follow up on someone or not. We didn't want to be intrusive, but wanted them to know we cared. Yet, the pattern I came to notice was that there was an unwritten rule that required us to let individuals make up their own minds about their involvement. They knew we were there and they were always welcome. The same principle applied later to support groups, the purpose of which was to provide a venue for people to share their feelings, experiences, fears, or grief, unlike the care teams set up to help people with AIDS. Over time, this came to include people with HIV/AIDS, caregivers, family members, and anyone else infected or affected by the illness.

Now, Steve! He and I became fast friends, but not before I had formed a close bond with Ken due to a greater similarity in age. Steve let me know that his first impression of me came partly from my dark hair and olive complexion, but mostly from the black T-shirt I was wearing at the first gathering of our new team. It was in a church where a large group of gays were members. The church subsequently became involved in housing an AIDS day-care center, dental clinic, and support network.

My T-shirt made reference to sailing on San Francisco Bay, and Steve made the assumption that I was a "Greek dyke." I had no complaints about his perception except that it was wrong. Actually, printed on the shirts were my company's initials (the company was also known by those initials), and the shirts were given to anyone who had sailed on the boat we rented for the annual interior designers' show held every year in San Francisco. My boss, instead of staying at a hotel to attend the show, would dock the large sailboat at Pier 39, bunk the few employees he had chosen to go with him, and then entertain vendors and other show attendees by sailing across the bay to some fine restaurant in Tiburon or Sausalito.

Steve worked for a very large insurance company, which moved him to their Dallas office after a few years. But he still called me every Friday afternoon, even though it was no longer to ask me what we could do together that weekend.

When he was still with the team, we became very supportive of each other—not only with our teamwork, but also in our personal lives. Steve was in a relationship that was faltering due to his partner's departure to work in Paris. We talked endlessly on the phone, had dinner together numerous times, and loved going to movies. Before we went anywhere, his way of asking me was, "Sound good?"

It always sounded good to me. I was happy to be with him. He was my son's age, he was personable, and he was very reliable—for a while.

Before we had all come to know each other and to embark together on what we presumed would be a brief journey, we sat at the training session that Sunday afternoon in December 1983, sharing our individual reasons for being there, and something about ourselves. We repeated the same role-playing exercises I had participated in before, and after a one-day orientation, we supposedly had learned *everything* we needed to know—at the time—and we were ready for the trenches.

1983

6.
Backing Up a Little

I had been determined to read George Orwell's *1984* before it lost its social and literary impact. In 1981, at the time of my Christmas vacation to Bass Lake, near Yosemite, with Gary and his lover (also named Gary), I still had two years to take care of that. I took the book along on our trip that year, planning to read it when I was curled up in front of the fire in our cozy cabin in the woods.

We left San Francisco as planned, but our schedule was interrupted by an unexpected snowfall that detained us in a tiny town along our route. The snowplows had strategically stopped their work adjacent to a motel, leaving us and other travelers facing a wall of snow that wouldn't be cleared until the next day. After checking into the motel, we made the most of our delay by renting cross-country skis from the motel's ski shop. Inquiring of the proprietress where we were allowed to ski, she replied, "Anywhere you want to."

We couldn't distinguish the highway from the fields, with the blanket of white stretching into a panoramic view of the countryside. I had never before entertained the thought of skiing, but I wouldn't consider putting a damper on either our vacation or my relationship with the Garys. Struggling to stay vertical was my biggest challenge, and I silently wondered at the purpose of cross-country skiing. At least if you were going downhill, you would feel the exhilaration of the wind against your face. But this falling down and twisting and turning to get up was exhausting and frustrating. A few years later, I would be introduced to downhill skiing and would feel much more productive. At least I would be going somewhere.

The next morning, while enjoying breakfast at the motel coffee shop, we were looking out the window at the snow piled on the roof of the building next door. Just as we were contemplating the load that roof could bear, the snow let go and went sliding to the ground. If anyone had been standing there at the time, we would have had to mobilize a rescue effort. For me, these recollections are memorable because so much of my life has been spent in the southwest, where the heat goes on for most of our year. The beauty of California is a large part of the magic that being with Gary provided me. He was in love with the place and wanted to share it with me, just as he loved sharing "his" city, San Francisco.

Due to the snow delay, with the road climbing into the fog, we arrived at Bass Lake after dark. With one Gary driving very slowly and the other keeping him apprised of where the edge of the road was, we finally arrived at our cabin. We set up housekeeping, cooked a turkey with all the trimmings, drank Baileys Irish Cream with eggnog, and lazed by the fireplace. During the next few days, we trekked through the snow, making snow angels and building snowmen as we went. We hiked up to the waterfall at the peak of the trail, with me falling behind while Gary and Gary went on without me. Every so often, they stopped, turned around to see how far behind I was lagging, and waited for me to catch up to them. As soon as I approached, they resumed walking. I wasn't getting much relief at those rest stops, so I was very happy when it was time for a trail mix break. They both were obviously quite healthy.

Each night of our four-day stay, I read the book,

determined to prepare myself for the approach of that *dreaded* year. I continued to carry a long-held trepidation about the actual 1984. But this trip ushered in 1982, before anyone had heard a word about a thing called AIDS.

1981

7.

Arthur

George Orwell notwithstanding, in 1983, during my third vacation with Gary since his move to California—this time to Lake Tahoe for skiing and to Disneyland for warming up—we returned to San Francisco to ring in the New Year, 1984. We had planned to continue a tradition we had begun the year before by spending the evening in the hot tub, indulging in rum-filled chocolates. But there had been a power outage while we were away, so the plan was scrapped. To at least acknowledge the New Year, we went out in the street with noisemakers, came in, and went to bed. Two days later I was back home.

The next morning, a phone call from Ken informed me that we were to meet in a few hours to help our very first client move from a small garage apartment to his own place. The downstairs garage apartment was rented by Joe, a friend of Arthur's who had been kind enough to let Art stay with him for a short time. It was so cramped that there was hardly room for one, much less both of them. But that was what the guys were doing in those days, helping each other as much as they could. This new illness had anybody who cared, and saw what was happening around them, coming to the aid of their friends who were sick. Who knew that many of them, too, would soon cross over from the "worried well" to those who had It, as the illness was then called.

Ken informed me, "We're meeting over at Joe's at two o'clock this afternoon to move Art to his new apartment."

"Does that mean we're a team?" was my not-so-ready reply. I was willing, but apprehensive of what was to be the beginning of my new destiny.

"Yes, we're a team."

The five of us (Chris having already dropped out) showed up at Joe's, bumping into each other while carrying a minimal amount of furniture (and not much else) that was identified as Art's belongings. Ken's friend Rick, who worked for the telephone company, joined us and installed Art's telephone. Rick lived with Ken as a roommate and was a recipient of Ken's early caregiving. Ken was such a good organizer, as we learned that day, that it was inevitable that he would be selected as our Team Leader. At any given time in the next six and a half years, he was caring for and/or opening his own home to someone with AIDS who had nowhere else to go.

There were many people who offered their homes to those who, for any number of reasons, didn't have a place of their own. It might have been that because of their illness, they could no longer work, and therefore had no means of supporting themselves. Or perhaps their family had disowned them, making it impossible to turn homeward for assistance. They might have lost their job because their employer fired them upon learning of their health status, or simply because they were gay. Sometimes, a lover had abandoned them because of their HIV/AIDS status; often, the lover would eventually be diagnosed. Explanations of why the gay community found itself itinerant were not in short supply.

We were known as a Care Team, and the services we provided were varied—from grocery shopping to cooking, doing laundry, or cleaning the house. Providing transportation to medical appointments or to attorneys' offices, walking the dog, going out for meals, or just socializing were a few of the activities we did to alleviate some of the stress our clients were feeling. While it removed the autonomy they had once enjoyed, at least they knew that their basic needs were being addressed.

Joe was not a member of our official team, but fit himself in by helping wherever he could. He was a professional massage therapist who donated his time and services at the hospital bedside of any AIDS patient who wanted a full or partial massage. He continued for many years to be unofficially involved with our group.

The team took turns visiting Art and carrying out any requests he had, such as washing the sheets ("Be sure to use bleach, and oh, be sure to wear latex gloves"). Art was taking care of us at the same time we attended to his needs. One evening after I had gone to the gym, I called him to see if he wanted company. When I arrived, he was busy hooking up his IV, having been instructed by his assigned nurse at the hospital. After he completed that project, we decided to watch TV, but soon found that there were no programs we really wanted to see. Since we hadn't actually gotten to know each other, we began exchanging pleasantries. Only a few minutes had gone by when I noticed blood backing up into his IV line. Until then, I thought I was doing a pretty good job of hiding my fear of what I had gotten myself into, but at that moment, my heart started pounding. What do I do now? I didn't have to do anything; Art was already paging the nurse for help. All he had to do was get another IV tube from the large box furnished by the hospital and he was back in business. Then we agreed to play board games the next time and go to movies. That would be easy.

But there was no next time; at least not for movies or playing games. Cecil had promised Art that he would take him to the grocery store the next day. As it happened, there was also no next day for shopping. Ken called to tell me that Art had pneumonia, and that Cecil had taken him to the hospital instead of the grocery store. Cecil didn't take him to the VA Hospital where he worked; Art wasn't a veteran. He went to MD Anderson, the one that specialized in the research and treatment of cancer, and had taken on the ominous challenge of treating the city's AIDS cases. Perhaps their early perception of the epidemic was that it would be short-lived, or that a treatment and cure would soon be found. What was short-lived was the hospital's capacity to deal with the quickly growing AIDS population.

Our mode of caregiving changed quickly, from household helpers to greeters. Art's parents were coming to town and we needed to prepare the one-bedroom apartment for them. That meant clearing out any trace of questionable reading or smoking matter that might have had to be accounted for. Buddy and I agreed that I would take the laundry to my house, so we could put clean sheets on Art's bed for his parents. There was only one set in the apartment. He would stay and screen the "matters" that were most likely something that I—as a parent, and a woman—wasn't supposed to see. Meanwhile, Joe went to the airport to pick up Art's mother and father. I returned around midnight and got the linens on the bed just minutes before they arrived. While I was gone, someone else had brought snacks and drinks, and we all sat around the table getting acquainted and preparing for the days ahead.

Art's parents were very grateful to us for helping Art, but did not seem to fully understand that what had afflicted their son was somehow related to his being gay. For the next two weeks, we all took turns going to the hospital, suiting up in identical yellow paper clothes—paper shoes and all—which were neatly stacked inside the first isolation room that led to the *really* isolated inner room. We were instructed by the nursing staff in the Intensive Care Unit to be sure to leave the hospital garb inside the room, lest it contaminate anyone on the outer side of the heavy glass window. It took many months before anyone gave consideration to the fact that the person in the bed, hooked up to a ventilator to stay alive, was the one who needed protection. There, Art was connected to a ventilator that prevented him from speaking to us, but not from communicating. He wrote notes on a large pad of paper and used hand gestures. It took two of us, Ken and I, playing "Twenty Questions" to guess that the foot movements and hand pointing didn't mean he wanted his feet rubbed, but that he wanted us to pull the covers up for him.

Within days, thirty-two-year-old Art was gone, and it was time for a funeral at the Catholic Church and for company at the apartment. A photograph of Art, taken before we knew him, had been placed next to the guest book before the funeral service. What a handsome young man! Could this have been the same gaunt person we had known, with the burr haircut, who looked so very fragile? It was. I knew then that I was in for a lot more heartbreak, and would need all the determination I could gather to continue my service.

Friends of Art's showed up at his apartment after the service; people who had not made an appearance during the six weeks we had come to know him. They spoke about different times in their lives that they had shared with him. They cried, they ate, and they talked among themselves. Some went roller-skating in the street outside the apartment. The whole thing was so new to everyone; it was difficult to comprehend that it was afflicting otherwise healthy people whose lives were much like ours. It was no longer a case of "them" and "us"—it was all "us." Art's mother asked me if everyone assembled in Art's small apartment was gay, and I said that it was likely most of them were. She replied that they really had a problem. I wondered whether she meant that they had a problem because they were gay, or because they might become infected with the virus. I also didn't know if she was being sarcastic, or whether she was really concerned for the health of the gay community. I didn't ask her to clarify her remark, partly because I thought it might be negative and I didn't want to hear that, but mostly because she had enough to cope with right then.

I was the last one to leave Art's apartment the night of the funeral. His parents were preparing to return to their New England home to bury their son's ashes on New Jersey soil. They wanted me to take some of the flowers home, along with a memento "to remember Art," as if I might not otherwise. I chose the large green plastic tumbler he had kept by his bedside, filled with water so that he could take his medicines. It stayed six years in my kitchen cabinet before I realized it would be a perfect water container for my watercolor painting class, so I am always reminded of Art when I paint. Just as I was saying goodbye to Art's parents for the last time, his mother said, "Don't you want anything else?"

I picked up a paperback copy of Arthur Miller's *The Crucible*, and went home.

1984

8.
Bob

The team was advised to take a break after Arthur's death at the end of February before we could be assigned another client. It was supposed to help us absorb the sadness and "process" the grief. But all too soon, on Sunday, April 30, we assembled at an upstairs garage apartment to meet Bob and his parents, who had come from Missouri, and Bob's partner, Truman. Bob was a dark-haired imp with a twinkle in his eyes; the expressive brown eyes blinded by cytomegalovirus (CMV), an infection contracted only months before. Until he became ill, he was an illustrator, executing exquisitely detailed pen and ink drawings of plant life for textbooks, covering a wide range of flora. Pen and ink must have been his forte, because that was the medium used in most of the drawings I saw at his home. It was pen and ink that he used so well in the drawing of a small boy playing with a toy train, which Truman later gave to me. I cherish the drawing, but I don't need it to remember Bob.

Truman was over six feet tall, with thick black hair and blue eyes. What a combination that was. And what a combination the two men were, for Bob was just a little over five feet in height. Truman was a theater teacher at a small-town high school; if any of the faculty or—perish the thought—the principal had found out that he was gay, he would have lost his job, even though he had repeatedly been honored by the faculty. He was a teacher who let his students know at the beginning of the semester that he would be tough but fair. Within a week or two after school started in the fall, the kids tested him and discovered he meant exactly what he said. Yet, after they graduated, many of them would return to visit him, or stayed in touch by mail. However, when it came to faculty, gay was not the thing to be in his small town.

So there we were, meeting our second adopted family whose lives had been thrown off track by the insidious virus. No cures, not much medication available, and all of us knowing what the outcome would be. Bob, besides wearing a T-shirt and sweat pants, had on the biggest fuzzy tiger slippers I had ever seen. When I told him how I admired them, he blurted out, "I'm so embarrassed! I forgot I had them on. Why didn't somebody tell me?"

The poor guy wasn't used to not seeing, but that was only the beginning of what we would soon find out was part of Bob's not-so-subtle sense of humor.

When Bob's parents returned home to Missouri, Truman doted on Bob, in addition to doing all of the cooking, housekeeping, and the many tasks necessary to maintain a household. It was no wonder he needed help from the AIDS Foundation, as he had to fit those activities into his teaching schedule, in addition to taking Bob for treatments and tests at the same hospital where Art had died two months before. Because he was spending long hours at school designing and building sets, Truman requested a transfer to the English Department for the coming school year, in order to minimize his time away from Bob.

During the next few weeks, I got to know Bob and Truman by running errands for them. I returned books to the library and shopped for their groceries, but the big project came about when the AIDS Foundation asked Ken if he knew someone who could help Truman build a staircase handrail inside the two-story garage apartment. The ground level, which served as Truman's workshop, would eventually become a cozy living room, with one whole wall from floor to ceiling covered with built-in bookcases that held Truman's huge library. But at that time it housed Truman's tools, which included a large table saw. Truman had been remodeling the place and had had to put the project on hold because of his new, busier-than-ever schedule.

Ken, knowing that I worked at an interior design firm and had access to the names of woodworking contractors, called me first. I, in turn, asked my boss, Richard, if he would do a favor for me. His degree at Pratt Institute in Brooklyn had been in industrial design.

"Sure," he said.

"You didn't even ask what it is," I told him.

"So, you asked for a favor. What is it?"

I explained to him the danger of Bob's falling off the edge of the unfinished staircase if he didn't have something to hold on to, and soon! The following Saturday, Richard and I were at the apartment with a tape measure to take dimensions: vertically, horizontally, and diagonally. We came there with our usual vocabulary used for working together when I was helping him with such projects, which was not uncommon. So "the dumb end of the tape" explains what my role was, just hanging on to the thing while he measured.

I was sitting on the top stair while he was measuring this and that, and I asked, "Do you want me to hold the dumb end yet?"

"No, not yet," he called up from the first landing of the staircase.

Bob had been sitting on the couch next to me and took his cue.

"When you get down to needing a blind man, let me know."

That afternoon, Richard and I were off to the lumberyard. I was reveling in the incongruity of riding down the street holding on to a load of lumber through the sunroof of a Porsche 911. Once we started using the table saw and fitting the sections together, throwing sawdust all over everything in the room, Truman stood near us, eating a bowl of cereal and watching in awe at what was taking shape. I realized that Richard had never discussed his design of the handrail with Truman; he just started building it. Occasionally, Truman left us to work in the basement while he took Bob to the hospital outpatient clinic for his checkups. During the next few weekends, as the project moved forward and was coming to an end, I noticed that whenever Truman led Bob down the stairs, with Bob holding onto Truman's arm and Truman whispering quietly, "Step, step, step," Richard stopped what he was doing and turned to watch this ever-so-subtle expression of love. I believe the experience was, for Richard, the beginning of at least a small part of his understanding that gay relationships are not very different from any other.

When the handrail was complete, Truman claimed that it was exactly what he had had in mind, and would have done if he had built it himself. I feel positive he didn't just say that to make Richard feel good. After all, it was designed and built by a professional industrial designer.

A few weeks later, the AIDS Foundation sent a letter of appreciation to Richard, which he nonchalantly tossed into the wastebasket. When I asked why he didn't keep the letter, he just said, "I didn't do it for that."

He was obviously moved by what he had seen, and that was his reward. As time went on, he continued to learn from my experiences and involvement.

One Saturday night, Ken and the other men in our volunteer group felt that Truman needed a break, and asked me to stay with Bob while they went out to dinner. I was happy to oblige, but I was also apprehensive. What if he got sick and I didn't know what to do? Mostly he slept, but around midnight, just as I had drifted off to sleep on the couch, Bob called out, "Are you awake?"

"Well, yeah, I am now. What's up?"

"Would you come in and talk to me?" Bob asked.

While I massaged his back, Bob cried that he didn't mind having a babysitter, but he didn't think it was fair for Truman to go out and not even ask if it was all right with Bob. At that moment, I realized how often other people would make decisions on behalf of someone who had lost the power and autonomy they once had. It was a sad time for Bob and a learning experience for me. I had no idea at the time how often that thought would come into play in my future as a volunteer—or, for that matter, as a participant in life.

On Sunday night, May 27, Bob had a grand mal seizure at home and was taken by ambulance to the hospital. From then on, one infection after another invaded his tiny body. The day after his admission to the hospital, the neurologist allowed me to stay in the room while he asked Bob a battery of questions, such as what day of the week it was, what holiday were we observing, how many nickels in a dollar? He asked the college Bob had attended, to which Bob proudly answered that he was a big football fan of the University of Missouri Tigers. Why else would he have been wearing those big tiger slippers?

Bob was doing great until he was asked, "Does a helicopter feed its young?"

Bob answered, "No."

Good for you, Bob, I thought. The doctor thought he was going to trip you up.

"Why doesn't a helicopter feed its young?"

Unfortunately, Bob's answer was, "Because a helicopter is a machine, not a building."

My heart sank.

Surgery was called for, after CT scans revealed the cause of the seizure. Even though Bob was well aware of his own health status, the doctors wouldn't accept his authorization for the surgery—not because of misidentifying the feeding habits of helicopters, but because he was on medication and, apparently to them, unable to make a rational decision. Yet, Bob was the one who provided his parents' ten-digit phone number—from memory—for the doctors to call for the permission they needed. God forbid that they should accept Truman's authorization; he wasn't considered "family."

After the surgery, Bob had to endure rounds of chemotherapy, which, not surprisingly, caused his hair to fall out. Truman kept pulling the pillow out from under Bob's head to brush the accumulating hair from it. It happened one too many times for Bob. He finally shouted, "I can't understand why you're so damned preoccupied with my pillow!"

A few days later, Truman, thinking that Bob would prefer to sleep on his own pillow instead of hospital issue, brought one in a designer pillowcase. When Truman wasn't there, Bob asked me which pillowcase he had. When I described it to him by pattern, color, and designer, Bob fussed, "That Truman! He knows I can't stand that one."

Obviously, whether or not he could see was not the point.

In fact, he made that even plainer to me a few days later, when I appeared in his room completely covered in the traditional yellow paper uniform—shoes, pants, shirt, and mask. Trying to make light conversation, I blurted out without thinking, "I guess we all look alike in these get-ups."

To which Bob, not missing a beat, replied, "It doesn't make any difference to me. I can't see you anyway."

My embarrassment immediately brought another new revelation to me: when you make that kind of faux pas, you just apologize and go forward.

Once Bob healed from the surgery, he endured at least four more setbacks. After they were more or less under control, Bob, in a long-distance phone conversation with his sister-in-law, was thrilled that he was "all better" and announced cheerfully, "Hey, Roxy, all I have now is AIDS!"

Things were not really that much better. In fact, it soon became necessary to outfit Bob with a condom catheter, as he became too weak to walk to the bathroom—and then too weak to use the portable urinal. The nurse, in ordering one to be sent up from the supply room, called out loudly to the staff at the desk, "I need a condom catheter in Room 235. Small."

Poor Bob, embarrassed by the announcement, complained, "Great! Did you have to tell the whole world that I wear a size small?"

Someone being with Bob in the hospital was crucial; some family members were coming from out of town but had not yet arrived. Truman had to finish out the spring semester, and for his sake, the team agreed to take shifts staying with Bob, because he began slipping into long periods of sleep and we didn't want him to be alone. One evening after work, I raced to the hospital, arriving in Bob's room only eight minutes after

I had left my office, but found Bob sound asleep. Not wanting to disturb him, I stood by his bedside for a few minutes and decided to quietly slip out of the room. Feeling uncomfortable about having left Bob like that, I confided in Gary, the therapist. He suggested that if it happened again, I would have nothing to lose by speaking to him, telling him I had come by to see him and would return at another time. If he heard me, fine. If not, it wouldn't do any harm. That was a valuable piece of information. Little did I know on how many occasions in the future I would put it to good use.

It was a difficult thing Truman felt he had to do, having Bob sign over power of attorney, but it was necessary in order to avoid greater complications later. Bob was totally agreeable to it, so that Truman could take care of financial matters while Bob was still alive. Since he didn't have a will, it was simpler and gentler to face those things with Bob participating. I obtained a power of attorney form from a lawyer who was apparently too busy or careless to provide a document that had not already been used. I don't mean that the format had been used; the actual piece of paper had previously been completed and made usable again by a generous application of whiteout. It was so lumpy and thick that even a sighted person would have had difficulty signing their name on it. But Bob and Truman wanted to get the matter moving along, so no one took the time to make a photocopy that would provide a clean, blank original. With pen at the ready, Bob asked me to place his hand on the line to get his signature properly positioned. With that small task completed, he asked me how it looked. How could I have said anything but "great" when I saw his name written at a perfect forty-five-degree angle across the line? I notarized it and gave it to Truman. As I had feared, the simple, questionable-looking document was scrutinized by the first person it was submitted to for action. Bob's banker called me, as the notary public, at the hospital, to ask about its legitimacy. He was quite apologetic when I explained its origination. After that, business was transacted and we had no more problems with that aspect of Bob's desires on this earth. He was still in the hospital and the flimsy threads of his life were rapidly disintegrating.

The next week, new infections set in and it was decided that Bob's family should be called to come back—possibly, and as it turned out, for the last time. Someone had to go to the airport to pick up Bob's brother and sister-in-law.

"I'll go," I said, without hesitation.

I made a sign with their names on it to hold at the arrival gate, so they could identify me. I had volunteered to be their airport greeter when it became apparent that we were mobilizing for another stage of Bob's life path. I could have gone without the sign, as his brother, John, looked so much like Bob that I would have recognized him immediately. I don't know why I had previously been embarrassed to do such a thing as hold a sign like that. But this time, almost everything I did had a built-in fervor. It was well rewarded when John and Sharon came through the gate, saw the sign, and ran toward me. They were effusively grateful and, like Arthur's family, were very compatible with our little group and bolstered our spirits, while I thought it was part of *our* job to support *them*. Most notably, they were completely supportive of Bob and Truman, pouring out their love without a trace of homophobia or fear. The remaining days of Bob's life were filled with quiet visits to his bedside as he slowly gave up his struggle. Maybe it was because his family was with him and Truman; more likely, it was because he was tired. He told Truman that his own death was easier for himself than for Truman, because Truman had to keep going.

Ken called me at work when Bob died. It was June 26, one month from the Memorial Day when he had been unable to remember a small detail for the neurologist. Truman had called Ken and wanted us to go to the hospital to see Bob for the last time. I expressed to Ken my hesitation to go. I had never before seen a person who had just died, but I told myself that I shouldn't decline. I felt that this would be a milestone for me, having never had the experience. But it was not to be the last. We stood watch over Bob until we were asked by hospital personnel to remove his things from the room. It took a long time to pack his personal belongings, and even longer to load all the flowers and tokens of friendship that had accumulated in that hospital room during June of 1984.

The hospital chaplain was a Catholic priest who had become a friend to Bob and Truman. He had visited Bob in the hospital many times and, at Bob's request, recited the 23rd Psalm with him. Father Zack had made a noble sacrifice by reciting the psalm according to Bob's Protestant version of it. It was still recognizable as the 23rd Psalm, but Bob had taken the liberty of changing the wording to suit himself. Now, Father Zack was conducting a simple ceremony in a small park in the heart of the city. Unknowingly at the time, Father Zack's words of comfort were to become the mantra in the circle I traveled for the next few years, citing Ecclesiastes 3:1. "To every thing there is a season, and a time to every purpose under heaven: A time to be born, and a time to die…"

A toy stuffed tiger was there to represent Bob's fierce allegiance to his alma mater, the University of Missouri, and I smiled as I remembered his big fuzzy slippers.

***

Since Truman had stayed friends with Bob's care team after Bob died, and he and I had formed a very close bond, it was natural for him to join us in social activities, even though he wasn't up to becoming a volunteer. He would have been great serving on the Speakers Bureau, putting to good use his professional speaking voice, but he preferred to let that talent remain in the classroom.

Because of his grief over losing Bob, Truman was in no mood to go out with other men, so I was the lucky recipient of his charming company. From the day after Bob's family left town, Truman and I began to see each other frequently. We went to dinner, movies, and sometimes a play. Almost every night, we found different places to have dinner. Every Saturday night, he would take me to one of the popular gay bars, where there was always a crowd of young men drinking and dancing to the country and western music. Sometimes there was a live band and sometimes a jukebox, but there was always an enthusiastic group of men on the dance floor. A new revelation for me was that there was also a crowd of married men who were "out with the boys," but not the boys their wives thought they were out with.

In August of that year, I had had surgery on both feet, and tromped around with Truman in those terribly clunky surgical shoes. I stayed at Truman's house during my recovery and he was very attentive to my needs, even though for him it recalled the heartbreaking memories of caring for Bob. He kissed me gently on the cheek each morning as he left for work and again when he returned. He prepared meals for us both, and when I was able, we returned to the bar. He vowed to get me out on the dance floor once the shoes went, but I was spared the embarrassment I knew would be mine if Truman got his way. I never knew how to dance in the first place.

We saw *Torch Song Trilogy*. It provided a lot of laughs, but in the scene in which the mother, visiting her gay son whose lover has died, claims, "You don't understand widowing," she goes on talking on top of his grief by describing her own after her husband had passed on. At that point, I heard deep, low sobs. Glancing to my left, I saw Truman's upper body shaking in the throes of emotion; he was trying valiantly to not be caught showing his feelings. By then, I couldn't hold back my own tears.

One evening, Truman called to ask if it was all right if we didn't have dinner together that night. He explained that he felt it was time for him to begin life on his own. It was fine with me, so I prepared my own dinner and was just beginning to dig in when the phone rang. It was Truman, his usually booming bass voice sounding small and meek.

"Is it too late to change my mind?"

He wasn't yet ready to leave the security of our unconditional acceptance of each other. Within a few months, sooner than what I would have preferred, he announced to me that he needed to begin socializing again with men, so we began to drift away from each other.

1984

9.
Fred

The team didn't get a break after Bob died. We were already assigned to Fred while caring for Bob in his final days. Fred was an advertising manager for the slick-covered program given to opera, ballet, and symphony goers. He was somewhat of a snob, or so it appeared when we first met him. It was a Sunday afternoon, when Buddy had come to my house to help me in the yard. He was always willing to help, whether it was for someone with AIDS—as he had done when Arthur's parents arrived from out of town and he and I cleaned Art's apartment—or to lend a hand to a fellow volunteer.

We had planned to have dinner at my place, but before we had the chance to eat (because we were still working outdoors), Ken called. He said that we had to meet at Fred's apartment, because Fred had prepared dinner for us and was eager to meet his new team. Buddy and I dropped what we were doing and headed over there.

Fred had prepared the best-tasting black bean soup I've ever had, served with a dollop of sour cream in the center and topped with a small sprig of cilantro. My compliments to the chef were returned with, "Do you cook?"

Somehow, I sensed what Fred's next words would be when I answered, "Not much."

"Well, you'd better learn, so when you have to take care of me, you'll be able to cook for me."

I felt very intimidated by that remark, but met his other requests willingly. Fortunately, for both of us, the occasion never arose when I needed to cook for him.

There wasn't much to do for Fred before he went into the hospital for some tests, but I was given a long grocery list, which included yogurt ("Be sure to get the kind with live cultures.") and toilet paper ("Be sure to get white, and extra soft"). He was so specific about each item that I hesitated to make any decisions of my own if forced to by an absence on the store shelves of any of Fred's requests.

My only solo social experience with Fred was seeing a movie we had agreed upon without knowing anything about it, except that we assumed it was a comedy. Fred picked me up at my house. As I opened the door, the first words he spoke were, "Oh, you wore jeans. I was going to, but changed my mind. I thought it would be too casual."

Great! I was off to a good start. Once we were in the theater and the lights went down, I was recovering my composure and thinking we might still have a good time together. When the story line suddenly went from humorous to indecent, Fred commented, loud enough for more ears than mine, "Oh, it's a tits and ass movie."

Notwithstanding that observation, the movie didn't appeal to either of us, but as we discovered later, we were both politely deferring to the other by not suggesting that we leave. In an effort to compatibly salvage the evening, we had dinner in the same mall where the movie was showing. As uncomfortable as I was with my formidable new acquaintance, it appeared that Fred felt the same about his. He dropped his silverware—first the fork, then the knife. We struggled through conversation and I couldn't get out of there soon enough. Once I returned home and Fred had left, I wondered how I was going to calm down enough to fulfill my responsibilities as one of his caregivers.

Ken, Fred, and I went to dinner together while Fred was experiencing the fear of his inevitable and quickly approaching death. It wasn't long before he called me to ask how I dealt with depression. I frankly don't remember what I told him, but I do remember that he had suddenly carved a soft spot in my heart with that question, because depression was no stranger in my life. I must have suggested something worthwhile, because Fred checked himself into the hospital to be treated shortly after. He came through that period fairly quickly, which I could tell when I entered his hospital room and found him flipping through his Rolodex cards finding names of people to call. In fact, if he wasn't calling them, they were calling him, and I sat with him through those many conversations. Each time I tried to make my exit, he waved me back. By the time he was talked out, visiting hours were over and I left.

Ken's birthday was Friday, August 31, and to ensure a good turnout to celebrate it—being the half-century mark—he decided to host his own party. It would be at a small restaurant with a large back room, where the twenty-four invited guests could fit comfortably and privately. With Fred still in the hospital, it was uncertain whether he would be there to round out the even two dozen friends and co-caregivers. I received a call at work that morning from Ken, informing me—rather formally, I thought—"Fred won't be joining us for dinner this evening."

I asked him why, and he replied tersely, "Fred decided to die on my birthday."

It sounded funny to me, but I think Ken really believed it.

Gary was to arrive from San Francisco at midnight for a visit over the Labor Day holiday, so I asked Truman if he would ride with me to airport. He agreed, and after hugs all around—from Ken, Steve, Joe, and most of the rest of my unlikely social group—we left Ken's party. I was anxious to find out how my son was, after just having faced the loss of our team's third charge. Before his short visit was over, Gary had met most of my new friends and seemed pleased with my involvement with them.

1984

10.
Fund-raising

Funds were in short supply and coming up with ideas for changing that became the latest challenge. It was a brand-new cause for which no one had any experience.

A fund-raising drive, advertised as a "gay-rage sale", was held in the parking lot of Mary's, one of the popular leather bars in town, to raise money for McAdory House. One of the few volunteer attorneys installed shelves in Stone Soup, the AIDS Foundation's food pantry, located in McAdory House. It didn't matter that he was an attorney. He was doing what needed to be done. The first donation that he stocked on the shelves was a six-pack of Perrier water. He also became a daily visitor to the AIDS ward at the county hospital, where he was known as Dr. Donut because when he brought the sweet treats to the patients—whom he referred to as "munchkins"—he told them, "Take two of these and call me in the morning."

Mary's held the key to the one-room office in the bank building across the street, where our first small group of volunteers met. If anyone needed to get into the office, they had to first get the key from the bartender at Mary's, then cross the busy street to the foundation's little office.

A portion of bar's property, called Outback of Mary's, is the final resting place of the ashes of some of the first people in Houston to die from AIDS. There was no other place that would accept them for burial. Among them are the original owner of Mary's and his dog.

One of the most successful fund-raisers in those early days was called Shopping Spree for All. Foley's, then a division of Federated Department Stores, joined forces with the AIDS Foundation, to hold a mega-sale at the city's brand-new convention center, the same building in which the AIDS Quilt has been displayed so many times. It was a huge success, raising over $60,000. Many Foley's employees volunteered to work with the AIDS Foundation to prepare for the event. For many days prior to the big sale, we met at one of the Foley's warehouses to price every item. This would be no ordinary rummage sale, in that all of the merchandise was brand-new and had been donated by the manufacturers or by Foley's. Only the cost of the goods told the shoppers they were at a bargain sale.

During the set-up phase in the convention center, the department store employees who volunteered their time and expertise for the sale competed to have the best-looking department for their merchandise. There were no prizes for their efforts. They were simply caught up in the sprit of the event. Even the wife of Foley's president worked as a sacker, converting garbage bags to garment bags by punching a hole in the center of the sealed end and inserting the wire hanger through it to hold the garment. Men's sport coats sold for ten or fifteen dollars each. There were about 150 of them.

Before opening the sale to the throng of eager shoppers, a double line of people waiting to get in had formed around the huge building. Volunteers were allowed to shop before the general public. When the doors were opened to the huge crowd, they charged in like the running of the bulls at Pamplona. The plan was to hold the sale for two days, but so much merchandise sold on the first day that the organizers were debating whether or not to continue the next day—a Sunday—because there was so little merchandise left, but decided after all that they would. As the goods were sold from the expansive floor of the building, the store employees kept consolidating the merchandise so it retained the appearance of a department store, even though it was shrinking rapidly to the size of a boutique. The fixtures were removed to the dock, where they could be easily loaded onto the store's trucks, and by the time the sale was over, the disassembling job was complete. The original plan had been to drive the trucks onto the sales floor and load the remaining merchandise and fixtures. As it turned out, all that was needed to transport the few things that remained was the backseat of a station wagon. Even the leftover wooden hangers were sold.

Afterward, Jack, one of the other volunteers, and I went to dinner at Ken's favorite restaurant, our ritual Friday night hangout. It was the same place where I had been so many times before, with family members after the funeral or memorial service for their loved one. Jack was the same person who, four years after the Shopping Spree, invited me to be his guest at the Mayor's Volunteer of the Year awards dinner and the AIDS Foundation fund-raiser the following night, at which we were seated with Morgan Fairchild. There is more written about that later. On this particular day, we were exhilarated but exhausted. It seemed to us that there should have been a huge celebration, and our little get-together was something of a letdown after all the excitement we had experienced.

Note: At this writing, I have just learned of Jack's death. We had not only worked together as volunteers, but occasionally he would stop by my house for coffee after a dental appointment in my neighborhood. It was purely coincidental that we both used the services of the same dentist. When I had surgery, Jack provided transportation for me to my doctor's office. This was one example of how a network of friends was created out of the tragedy of AIDS.

1984

11.
Moving the Goalposts

B y the time of Gary's first visit since his diagnosis, a year and a half had passed and he was living his life happily and with no apparent effects of any viral activity. He had not begun taking any medication, as his physician continued the approach of monitoring his patient's condition rather than the lab test results. Besides, there were no treatments to prevent the depletion of T-cells or the escalation of the AIDS viral load. There was no AZT, no multitude of drugs from which to mix the limited number of cocktails. There was not even a way of knowing whether no treatment was ultimately safer and more productive than the use of drugs which eventually became available. At that time, the scientists had only just discovered that the havoc being wreaked was caused by a tricky little virus. But there was *always* the knowledge that the disease was incurable and would ultimately claim the lives of all who had inadvertently hosted the tiny intruder.

By this time, the AIDS Foundation had had more than a few executive directors, beginning with volunteers but eventually finding the need to hire professionals. Some had died, and some left for other reasons. It was a very difficult job, as there was neither precedent nor protocol to follow. Where could anyone have gained the experience to lead a group of volunteers who gave their best to meet the medical, financial, legal, and social needs of people who were suddenly thrust onto a minefield while simultaneously attempting to evade a barrage of deadly ammunition? Perhaps in the armed services, but this wasn't the army. It was an amateur group facing a quicksand pit teeming with a prolific, sneaky and elusive tiny virus, and no matter who inadvertently fell into it, they knew that they would be pulled under. Unbearable sadness consumed me every time I heard someone say, "I'm going to beat this." It was incomprehensible for all of us to accept that no one was exempt from his or her inevitable fate.

The first executive director was a handsome and outgoing young man named Gary. I liked having so many Garys in my life; he was the fourth. To hear or say the name, wherever I was, made me feel good. The evening of the same day I had met with him to introduce myself, we saw each other in the grocery store where many gay men shopped. It was more than a shopping experience; it was a social event. That must have been why Ken called it "Disco Kroger." When we approached each other that night, I said something to Gary that I thought was rather inane. But in the days, weeks, months, and years to follow, it carried a great deal of weight in my travels through the relationships I had formed with so many gay men. I said, "Just think, if we hadn't met this morning, we would be passing each other right now and wouldn't know the difference."

Gary agreed. He didn't find it inane. He said, "And we'll be seeing a lot more of each other."

He was right. We did see each other often, mostly at AIDS Foundation meetings, sometimes for dinner, and often at Disco Kroger. But not long afterward, he moved to Boston, his hometown. As I recall, he wanted to spend his last days near his father. *Gary's* last days, not his father's. He wrote to me one time and I answered his letter, but before another one from him could arrive, he, too, had lost his battle with AIDS. He was the first person I had known who had volunteered to help those in need but succumbed to his own private war.

1984

12.
Danny

Ken and I were having dinner in a popular restaurant next door to the counseling center, which was at the time almost single-handedly trying to help the gay community cope with their devastation. It was the place I had originally called, at the suggestion of Gary's doctor, to find out what I could do to get involved; the same place where the care teams met every week to discuss our work with the clients.

Ken recognized Danny, who was eating alone, and decided to introduce himself and me. Apparently, Danny was a community icon; a writer for the neighborhood's gay newspaper, a disc jockey in an infamous leather bar, and an actor of sorts. When we came to know him better, we learned that Danny prided himself on having been in a play with Katherine Hepburn, although he admitted that he had not been her leading man. He was very friendly to us, and since Ken was so good at putting himself into other people's lives, we were immediately in Danny's.

September 13 was Danny's fiftieth birthday, and he was delighted to have lived that long, considering his AIDS infection. His friends and bar coworkers threw a big party for him in the bar, at which he no longer worked. Of course, it was closed to the public that night. It probably would have broken the local fire code had there been any more people than those who showed up for the party. Because I felt out of place going to a leather bar, I called Danny that afternoon to wish him a happy birthday. I was surprised and flattered that he asked if I would be at the party. When I expressed my apprehension, he wouldn't hear of it and insisted that I attend.

The party turned out to be a fund-raiser for Danny's benefit, so whatever anyone had to offer for bid or contribution was gladly accepted. One good-looking young woman, who was a reporter for the same gay newspaper Danny worked for, strutted to the stage, grabbed the microphone, and announced that she would strip off her blouse and bra if someone would donate $100 to the cause. I was not only startled at her offer, but at a loss to see why anybody in a group of gay men would take her up on that. Much to my surprise, among the men approaching the stage with their offerings was one with a personal check he had written for the bargained price. Off came the blouse, then off came the bra, to the hoots and hollers of just about everyone in the bar. As she pranced about the stage, the reporter hollered back, "If you've got 'em, flaunt 'em." Not only was the party a huge success, but the monetary donation to Danny was sizable.

Danny soon lost his battle to reach his fifty-first birthday. Within a few months after the big party, he entered the hospital for the last time, and amid the huge array of flowers, balloons, gifts, and cards, he gave up the fight. We needed to prepare for another party of sorts. Rumors were floating around that no one in Danny's family cared what had happened to him, which was not at all true. At a large outdoor gathering at the plaza downtown across from the local concert hall, many of Danny's friends and acquaintances paid tribute to him. Joe had been instrumental in putting it together, as he had been a close friend of Danny's. In fact, Danny had called Joe's little apartment "home," and had slept on a mat on the living room floor. That began not long after our team had moved Arthur out of Joe's apartment to his own place, the first day our team met to begin our volunteer journey.

Before the formalities to honor Danny had begun, Joe approached me with Danny's brother, Frank, who had come to the service from California, representing the entire family because they could not all afford to attend. Joe wanted me to notarize a blank legal document for Frank on behalf of Danny. It would have been a power of attorney—which, even if Danny himself had signed such a document, would have been invalid after his death. A power of attorney is only effective during the life of the maker of the document. After their death, other directives come into play, such as a will, trust, or some method of executing the decedent's wishes. Frank needed to have been named as executor of Danny's will, or substitute trustee had there been a trust, neither of which existed.

Frank and Joe had planned to fill in the pertinent information after the fact. I don't know who was going to sign Danny's name. I would have willingly obliged if Danny had executed the document, but it was too late for that, so I refused to be a party to an illegal act. One of the duties of a notary public requires identification of the signer, so it would not be legal to notarize an unsigned document.

As soon as I had a chance to relate the incident to Ken, I asked his opinion. Fortunately, I thought, he agreed with my decision. Later that evening, as the same people and a few others met at a beautiful townhouse for the traditional celebration of life—which meant that food was served—I had just filled my plate when Joe backed me into a corner. Thumping his forefinger on my sternum, in an accusatory voice he shouted, "You! You!"

I was saved from any further humiliation by someone

offering a toast to Danny. At the same time, unbeknownst to me, the driver's side door of my car was being smashed by the Norwegian consul, who was just backing out of his garage across the driveway. With someone who witnessed the accident calling me outside to exchange insurance information, I was spared any further wrath from Joe.

1984

***

Frank lived in Davis, California, about fifteen miles west of Sacramento. When he invited me, during Danny's farewell gathering, to visit him any time I was in the area, I really didn't anticipate that happening. But a few years later, Gary and I were returning from a trip to Reno on Christmas day. When we stopped for gasoline on Highway 80, a straight shot from Reno to San Francisco, I realized we were in Davis, so I decided to call Frank. Assuming he probably had other Christmas activities to attend to, we did not plan to visit him, but just wanted to say hello by phone.

Frank insisted we drop by, as we were only about five minutes from his house. When we arrived, we could tell that he and his wife were preparing their holiday meal. The rooms were beautifully decorated and the aroma from the kitchen filled the house—and the table was set for eight.

I was very touched by Frank's invitation because even though he was in the midst of preparing for dinner guests, he and his wife took the time to welcome us into their home on Christmas day, offer us a cup of tea, and share some memories of Danny.

Frank told us that Davis had been enshrouded in fog for many days and that they had not seen the sun or sky for two weeks. As we headed out again towards Gary's home, we were very anxious to put the fog behind us. It was very disconcerting; giving us a feeling of being smothered by the enveloping gray mist. Finally, seeing a bright circle of sunlight in the distance ahead of us, we turned to each other and, in unison, said, "There really is a light at the end of the tunnel!"

13.
Moving through 1984

In the past, I had felt that it was going be a year of meaningful events. And it certainly was, but no one could ever have guessed that they would be anything resembling what lay ahead. Little did I know that there would be endless heartbreak. Yet, once I looked at the year in retrospect, it turned out to be what I considered the happiest year of my life. This was due, in large part, to my intense involvement in the fight against AIDS. But there had also been the accumulation of friends and activities offering more social activity than I had had up to that time. There were birthday celebrations, including my own, which was attended by ten men who joined me at a popular disco dinner club. I had never had an occasion like that in my life until the next year, when we did it again. During 1984, we took part in fund-raisers and walkathons, attended plays and parties, and often shared meals. In October, I attended a family reunion in Michigan. Unfortunately, Gary did not attend. He was in good health, but very busy with his job and other activities. As if the year hadn't already been memorable, in December, both Garys and I took a three-week trip to the Middle East, and spent the first week in Israel with family members who live there. Gary, knowing that some families reject their gay relatives, had written to them in advance, to be certain that his arrival with a male companion would not be unwelcome. Fortunately, his aunts, uncles, and cousins were very excited and eager to see all three of us.

On Monday, December 18, to begin our tour of Egypt, we rode in a modern, air-conditioned bus from Jerusalem to Raffiah, where the Egyptian border guards had some laughs at our expense. Before entering the country, we had to face the scrutiny of uniformed security soldiers, who made certain we were not trying to personally import forbidden cargo.

My son went first. Asked to spread the contents of his camera case, he dumped it all out on the table. The soldiers were satisfied until they questioned what was in the small paper wrappers. Gary answered, "Condoms."

"What is condoms?" they asked him.

"Rubbers," Gary replied.

"What? Rubbers?"

"For sex!"

"Oh! Ballunas!"

With that, the guard turned to his comrades, gesturing as if to blow up a balloon, but indicating that he understood exactly what Gary had been trying to tell him. Then he explained in Arabic what he had just discovered, and they all broke into laughter. All three of us were humiliated, particularly when, after that little exchange, the guard turned to me and asked, "American?"

"Yes."

More great laughter, and he ushered me through to the other side of the checkpoint. Having had their entertainment, they waved the other Gary through customs without question. Had they connected the fact that I was the mother of the man with the condoms, perhaps they might have realized what the condoms were actually for. They didn't even look at our passports.

Once inside the customs building, we were detained long enough to fend off the insistence that we exchange one hundred and fifty American dollars into Egyptian currency. We soon realized that the detainer was waiting for an under-the-table payoff, and we got away with paying him ten dollars American to leave us alone. Exiting the building after overcoming that hurdle, we were directed to a small restaurant for our first taste of Egyptian food before boarding our next mode of transportation. It was a hot little bus that traveled across the Sinai Desert, during which time the driver played audiocassette tapes of Arabic music while various groups of passengers countered with music from their own ethnic backgrounds. The aisle seats were fitted with hinges attached to two more seats, one on each side of the aisle, so they could be turned down to provide even more seating, which increased the already jam-packed travel arrangement. Add to this people shouting across the bus—from front to back, side to side, in multiple languages—to stay in touch with their traveling companions, and maintaining that chaos for the duration of the trip. We finally boarded the ferry that crossed the Suez Canal, and after another four hours crossing the Sinai, arrived in the heart of Cairo in time for five o'clock traffic. Considering it was the middle of December, it was beginning to get dark. To further the traffic trauma in Cairo was the lack of driving lanes and the occasional turning off of headlights to "save the energy of the car battery," as we were later told by one of our taxi drivers.

At the curb of what appeared to be an eight-lane traffic circle, the driver asked us to disembark because our hotel was out of the way for the majority of the other passengers. He got up from the driver's seat, exited the bus, and climbed onto the roof of the vehicle to retrieve our luggage from the heap that was piled precariously high atop the bus, barely remaining within the rails. Majestically placing our bags on the ground, he turned to leave.

"What are we supposed to do now?" we inquired.

"Take a taxi to your hotel. Welcome to Cairo."

By the time we arrived at our hotel, the Holiday Inn Giza, it was very dark. The bellman, after unloading our luggage in the room, showed us to our outdoor balcony. He pointed out the pyramids to us. We could see three small, triangular shapes in the distance, and marveled at how exciting it was to finally behold them. *The Pyramids!* There they were, way out there.

The three of us fell into our beds, exhausted from the very long trip. It was difficult to believe that in one day we had traveled on a modern air-conditioned bus; a tiny, jam-packed, hot and noisy bus across the desert; a ferry boat across the Suez Canal; and finally, the chenille-ball-fringed taxi to our destination.

I awoke the next morning to the sound of Gary's voice, loudly proclaiming, "Oh, my God!"

I ran from my bed to the balcony, to see the pyramids practically across the street from us. What we had seen the night before was not the entire structures far, far away, but the tops of them very, very close to us. We couldn't wait to get going.

We toured the city with our able guide, Meena; visited the Egyptian Museum, the permanent home of the full King Tut exhibit; some of the many mosques; and had lunch at the lavish Mina Palace, a hotel originally built to house the visiting dignitaries for the opening of the Suez Canal in November 1869. We walked, bent at the waist, through the tunnels of the

Great Pyramid at Giza, to observe the pharaohs' tombs—and, of course, saw the Sphinx. I couldn't resist the opportunity to ride a camel. Which smelled worse, the camel or its driver? I didn't know, but I certainly didn't want to leave Egypt without having experienced that ride.

On our fourth night in Egypt, we left Cairo by train, bound for Luxor. En route, I asked Paul Nelson, our travel guide, if there was a shower on the train. He replied, "No, this isn't the Orient Express."

Notwithstanding the lack of a shower, sleeping on the train was an exquisitely pleasant experience; hearing and feeling the steady rhythm of the wheels against the rails through a deep and peaceful night's rest.

In Luxor, we boarded the ship for our cruise up the Nile with Paul. His father was English and his mother Egyptian, so he had full command of both languages, and was therefore able to communicate with the individual guides at each of our destinations and convey their comments to us. We docked at places of interest along the route to see the temples at Edfu, Kom Ombo, the Great Temple at Karnak—and, of course, the Valley of the Kings. We approached the Esna locks during lunch, so the many passengers who wanted to go up on deck to witness the operation left their tables in the grand dining room. Not realizing the value of such a rare opportunity, I chose lunch. Gary, ever curious and eager to participate in such educational matters, was gone for the duration of the lunch period. I wish someone had nudged me to go, too.

A large party for the guests on the cruise was held on Saturday night, for which the on-board beauty salon offered free makeup and headdress for the women. Of course, the results were exaggerated, to make us look like Egyptian queens or the like. Gary converted his striped T-shirt into a headdress resembling that of King Tut's funerary mask. It was a stretch of the imagination, but with his gallabiya (commonly worn by Egyptian men) and other adornments, it was sufficient to qualify him for the dance contest. Only costumed guests were allowed to participate. The catch was that the only dance performed by each entrant had to be a belly dance. Since Gary was a ballet student, he merged the sound of the words "belly" and "ballet," and cleverly announced his dance. Much to his surprise and delight, he won the contest. The prize left a lot to be desired—a small wooden doll which resembled a Hassidic rabbi, a strange gift on an Egyptian cruise—but nonetheless, the glory was his.

As luck would have it, on our last night on the boat, I awoke at 3:00 AM with a queasy feeling in my stomach, less than ready for the big event we had all been anticipating— the highlight of the trip, King Tut's Tomb. Lying on the top bunk bed in our cabin, I debated for a while whether or not to disturb Gary with my problem. Finally, fearing the worst, I called out, "Gary." The two Garys leaped out of their beds and ran for a wastebasket, just in case. For the rest of the night, I agonized about having to leave the boat by 8:00 AM, as Paul, our guide, had said we must. A German tour group was going to be boarding at that time and we had to be on our way. Gary pleaded with Paul to let me stay, but it was impossible to accommodate us, as our schedule called for us to continue on. At the Valley of the Kings, I stayed behind on the bus as the rest of the group visited Queen Hatshepsut's temple near Luxor. I missed going there, as well as the Great Temple at Karnak. But I was determined to enter King Tut's Tomb, even if I had to die there. It was an unbelievable site. It appeared to have been renovated, but we were assured that the figures that graced the walls surrounding the sarcophagus remained intact from the day they were first put there.

Cruising as far south as Aswan to see the High Dam and Lake Nasser, from there anyone in the group who wanted to pay extra could take a short side trip by plane to Abu Simbel, to view the temple. It had been moved, piece by piece, and reconstructed at a nearby locale, in order to prevent it from being lost underwater once the high dam was built.

The official tour ended on Christmas Eve, but the Garys and I still had one more day in Cairo. On Christmas morning, Gary C. met some American expatriate friends for brunch, while my son and I walked what seemed like many miles from our hotel to the Cairo Museum. We spent more time than we had had on the tour with Meena to revisit the treasurers of Tutankhamen. We walked because we were tired of dealing with the haggling of taxi drivers who bid against each other for our fare.

We returned to the pyramids for a closer and longer look at the Sphinx, and took a leisurely walk around the area. However, we both had cultural lapses when we decided that five dollars was too much to pay for a tour of the royal funerary boat of Cheops. We climbed the pyramids and took pictures of each other, and only realized it was forbidden after we returned home. In the pictures, we were standing next to a sign which read DO NOT CLIMB THE PYRAMIDS.

We found burial sites of many unnamed Egyptians at a large area where ancient citizens, who did not rank pyramids or tombs, were laid to rest. Suddenly, we heard a voice call out, "Gary."

It was Gary C., who had managed to find us in that vast expanse of sand and multitude of tourists.

Our week in Egypt ended on Christmas night, when we

flew back to Israel for another week of traveling and visiting more relatives. One of the passengers on the El Al flight accidentally dropped a small rectangular object on the tarmac at the foot of the steps leading to the entry door of the plane. Armed Israeli soldiers converged on the item, and the flight didn't depart until after security personnel determined that it was merely a Beatles audiotape.

After seeing so much sand and dirt in Egypt, Israel appeared to have been washed clean while we were gone. The day after Christmas, with pilgrims still very much in evidence in Bethlehem, Gary explored the Church of the Nativity while I shopped in the town square. His reaction to what he saw was not quite what I had expected. "Hey Mom," he said, "I got to see the plastic Baby Jesus."

For many years, although I was not a member of the Christian faith, I had hoped someday to be able to visit the Holy Land, particularly Bethlehem—and more particularly at Christmastime, to perhaps gain a feel for the sanctity of the site. Hearing the Christ Child referred to as "plastic" forever removed the mystique for me, but we were there and it was out of my system.

New Year's Eve day, we left the airport in Tel Aviv for the long flight to Paris, and the even longer flight to New York. Throughout the flight, I wanted to talk to Gary about his health status, but he was tired, and I was hesitant. It was a lot easier to interact with other people about their health. As much as I cared about them, the undeniable bond with my own son was far more sensitive. Perhaps the others had similar feelings with me, only in reverse, rather than expressing themselves freely with their own parents. There was a delicate balance between showing intense interest in Gary's health, and trying to allow him to live his life without letting AIDS become the dominant force of his existence. Did I have the right to intrude on whatever he might have been thinking about, or wanted to think about, on that long flight across the ocean?

There is the mother-son relationship which, in its uniqueness, carries a variety of levels of closeness. Casual conversation was easy, although sometimes I felt that the topics I chatted about were beneath his dignity. But he was polite and often indulgent. The next level, meaningful exchange, was more satisfying to both of us. In the early days of Gary's diagnosis, I'm sure he felt not only obligated but eager to keep me apprised of his condition. After all, we were in it together. But as time went on, he retreated to his original response to questions about his health status: "I just wish someone would call and ask me to go out for a pizza." I believe that could be paraphrased to apply to his mother's inquiries: "Let's talk about something else." Then again, he was determined to protect me from worry and anxiety, and I genuinely believe that, for the most part, he felt he was doing the right thing by not giving me daily bulletins.

Much to our surprise and delight, we were the first ones at the luggage carrousel and got through customs without a hitch. We had two hours to wait for our connecting flights; the Garys to San Francisco and mine back home. From a pay phone in the airport, we made a Happy New Year conference call to a relative in New York, and then sat the rest of the time without making conversation. I wondered if and when the next time I saw my son he would still be alive.

I never finished reading the book *1984*. It didn't seem to matter anymore. For my team and me, our first momentous year was over.

1984

14.
A New Year—A New Beginning

As with any organization when it grows faster than it is capable of controlling, there was some amount of dissention within the group and some from without. At a business meeting held in the basement of the church where I had first met Steve, and where many of the AIDS Foundation's activities took place, I heard complaints about the financial statements of the foundation. I don't recall what the problem was, but I do remember that an accountant in attendance volunteered to review them and signed on to oversee such matters, thereby resolving that particular dispute. An audit was performed every year because the foundation had to be accountable to its donors.

Someone grumbled about one of the volunteer attorneys who served on the board of directors, but made it clear that he would not make any hospital visits. He had claimed that it was something he simply could not do. The grumbler felt that it disqualified him from serving on the board. I was outraged at the notion that he should not be allowed to serve because of his aversion to hospitals. I felt that he was performing a very valuable service to people with AIDS by preparing their legal documents, and assisting them with medical insurance problems, Social Security, and disability issues—all pro bono. How could anyone fault that? Each person had something to offer, and it all served for the good of the whole.

With a change of leadership, some of the activities were rearranged and reorganized because of the fast-growing number of people asking for many different services. Until then, five or six people formed a care team which helped their client with a variety of tasks. One day, one person might handle laundry duty or grocery shopping, or perhaps cook a meal for their client. The next day, another team member would drive the client to the doctor. Sometimes they worked in pairs, but there was usually a brief respite for each team member by spreading the tasks around. We were not medical personnel; we simply helped with typical, mundane chores.

The reassignment of team members was broken down into different categories of teams. The "A" Team consisted of those who helped out at the newly acquired McAdory House and Stone Soup. By a quirk of fate, when I first heard the address of the new hospice, I immediately recognized it as the first art studio of my former husband, a commercial artist. Upon entering the room where the food pantry stood, I couldn't help but think back to many years ago, when a colored chalk portrait of me, drawn at Knott's Berry Farm, hung on that very wall. Also, that the trip to Knott's Berry Farm was part of a family trip to Disneyland for Gary when he was a small boy of five. Now I was in that room again, after so many years, inadvertently because of Gary.

With the Buddy Team in place, each client was assigned one volunteer, known as a "buddy" from the "B" Team, who could be called upon to handle a variety of chores, or perhaps just to keep the client company. An effort was made to match the volunteer buddy to their client according to interests, personalities, and sometimes capabilities of the volunteer to accommodate particular needs. It was a one-on-one relationship, with the possibility of forming closer bonds of friendship and care. This reorganization became necessary because the number of clients was growing faster than their needs could be accommodated, and there were no longer enough volunteers to work in teams for the care of one person.

The third team was known as the Advocate Team. I wasn't feeling secure enough on my own to meet the known—or, heaven forbid, the unknown—demands of being a buddy, so I joined the Advocate Team.

As an advocate, my job was to respond to requests made either by a PWA (the newly coined term for a person with AIDS), his partner, or family. We were not to act as an advocate for anyone who did not ask for help through the foundation, so my assignments were delegated from headquarters. Often, I would be required to meet with the parents of someone who was in the hospital. The PWA might need financial assistance, help finding housing they could afford, or, for that matter, a place they would be allowed to live where they were accepted as a person with AIDS. Or they might have felt the need to move into the hospice, which was solely for people with AIDS. Sometimes, they just wanted to be assigned a buddy. After completing the intake forms indicating the requests of the PWA, the members of the Advocate Team met on Monday nights at the counseling center to present their cases to the Social Services Committee.

At that time, there were very few women involved in the program, probably because the majority of cases were affecting gay men and they were quite good at taking care of their own. At the time, being a parent who was the only one to date who had made the commitment—and particularly one who also had a son with the same illness—didn't hurt either. They wanted someone who could bridge the potential chasm between gay and straight, child and parent. It was flattering to know that I was entrusted with that awesome responsibility.

1985

15.
Time Passes Too Quickly

By the fall of our first year together, 1984, the original team had gotten very comfortable with each other. We had celebrated Rick's and my birthday in February, Ken's and Truman's in August, and Danny's in September. Some of the celebrants weren't our team members, and not all of the team's members observed their birthdays with us. I was pleased with myself in 1984 for having organized my own birthday gathering at a disco dinner club and having at least eight men agree to attend. I had never before been the honoree at such an event, albeit of my own making, so I repeated my self-indulgence in 1985. Many of the same invitees joined me that year, at a rather sedate restaurant; sedate only until the group began to sing to me and the other diners joined them. It was even more flattering that Joe and his partner, Tim, invited the group to their apartment for more revelry. By this time, months had passed since my unpleasant encounter with Joe after Danny's death. Actually, I had forgotten about it by the time I decided whom to invite to my birthday dinner. I was, at that time, more thick-skinned than I would eventually become. I would not have been able to continue with the never-ending frustration which goes along with AIDS if I hadn't learned to quickly pick up the pieces after a setback and carry on.

Only four of us from the birthday gathering accepted Joe's and Tim's invitation. Ken, his roommate Rick, Steve, Tim, and

I posed for a snapshot on the couch in front of Joe's tripod, with the Polaroid camera set on a timer to snap the photo in five seconds. Just as Joe ran to join the rest of us, his little fluffy dog jumped into my lap. The shutter clicked, and I was given the only print of a picture which would, in the not-too-distant future, come back to haunt me.

Even though we were not inseparable, our gang remained an intrepid band of theretofore unlikely companions. That is, until the Sunday evening I received a call from Truman informing me that Buddy had taken his own life. He had been intensely involved when the team prepared for the visit of Arthur's parents. When he had helped me with my yard work, he had given no indication of anything so dire that he would even contemplate suicide. I was dumbstruck at the news! How could he do that, and why? He wasn't even sick! At least, he wasn't sick with AIDS. Anyone who was physically healthy was supposed to cherish their life.

Apparently, Buddy's misery over his lost love was too great for him to bear. Buddy had come to me in the weeks before his death to seek my advice about his newly diagnosed liver ailment. I think he had finally been convinced that he was drowning his sorrows in the wrong river, a fairly steady stream of alcohol. He needed some tests run, and asked to borrow some money to pay for them. As far as I knew, that problem was behind him. Miller, his ex, called me to find out if Buddy had confided any secrets to me that might have revealed a reason for his actions. It was the first time I had spoken with Miller, although I had heard a lot about him, from Buddy's point of view. I had nothing to offer. I wished he had called me months before. The only thing I could think was, what a waste.

Buddy was gone, that was all I knew.

1985

16.
Tim

Although Joe was not a part of our team, he had become attached to us since our first assignment to Arthur, whom we had moved out of Joe's apartment on our first day of duty. He was apparently under tremendous pressure at that time. His partner, Tim, was failing fast. Tim, one of my birthday dinner invitees, worked at a large electronics store and knew all of the merchandise thoroughly. When my boss, Richard, told me that he was interested in purchasing a new television set, I recommended that he patronize the store where he could avail himself of Tim's expertise. We drove a long distance on the freeway until we found the place, but it apparently was worth it for Richard. The TV Tim recommended was by far not the least expensive, but he promised it would be worth the price. I have been glad to hear Richard, on occasion, tell me how pleased he is with that set, and it has been more than sixteen years since he bought it.

Not long after seeing Tim in action at his job, proudly displaying his knowledge of the merchandise, we learned from Joe that Tim was ill and his time to leave us was near. His family drove into town from up north to say goodbye. Each member had their own private audience with Tim, as all six or eight of them waited together in the small kitchen of Joe's apartment with Ken and Steve (two of my team members), and me. We had chosen to support Tim and Joe, not as AIDS Foundation volunteers, but as personal friends. One by one, Tim's family entered the living room where he lay on the couch, and spent a few minutes with him before they retreated out the front door to assemble in their van for the trip back home. Then it was our turn; Ken, Steve, and me. We were also invited to have one last personal visit with Tim. Of course, since we each spent that time alone with him, I had no way of knowing what Ken and Steve said, and I don't recall my own farewell, but I remember the feeling of incredible sadness at having, once again, to say goodbye to someone who had become dear to me. It was a touchingly dramatic occasion, which occurred only that one time. I'm not sure I could have endured participating in another parting ceremony such as that. As we left for the evening, we knew it would be our final farewell to Tim, at least while he was alive.

The following weekend, Joe hosted the customary celebration of life for Tim at the Body Positive reception room. Funerals were not the only way to say goodbye to someone who had died. Many gays had chosen not to belong to any organized religion. They might have been disinherited by their family or their family's religious group. There were many cases of disenfranchisement—although thankfully, Tim was not one of them. That didn't mean that *our* community (for I was now considered a member of the AIDS community) couldn't honor the life and value of the deceased, so that was what we did. We celebrated his life.

After the capacity crowd had had their fill of finger sandwiches, chips, dips, soft drinks, and sweets, we all paid our tributes to Tim, with Joe waiting to speak last. After talking about his love for Tim, and Tim's love for cars and things electronic, Joe pointed to the sixty-something-year-old table radio that had struck me as being incongruously placed among the other objects in the room. He announced that because of Tim's involvement with radios, that was where his ashes had been placed, and he had been inside the radio all day so that he would not be left out of his own party. Needless to say, that broke the somber mood; we had to laugh to keep from crying. That dying business was getting old.

1985

17.
Rick

Rick, the telephone company worker who had installed Art's phone in his new apartment, lived with Ken. When I first met them, I thought they were a couple; but, as mentioned before, Ken was always looking out for someone, whether it was by giving them a roof over their head or by doing a little prescription recycling. Though illegal as it may have been, Ken did his part to make sure that unused prescription drugs did not go to waste. The few available medications were extremely expensive, and many of the people who needed them simply could not afford them.

Rick was the proud owner of an old, blue, beat-up Spider convertible that badly needed selling. It could redeem itself if its existence was transformed into cash. Since Ken's apartment complex furnished only one parking space to its occupants, and since Rick was not known by the management to be an occupant, it became necessary for him to surreptitiously move the car from one unauthorized parking space in the neighborhood to another. During the period of this annoying inconvenience, Rick was attempting to find a buyer for the little car. When that was accomplished, he was required to furnish transfer papers for the vehicle, which included the properly signed and notarized title, in addition to an application for new title to be signed by the purchaser.

Ken, once again jumping in to aid in Rick's progress,

asked me to bring my notary seal and go with him to a gay bar to have the appropriate documents signed by the bartender, the lucky new owner of Rick's Spider. Since he worked such odd hours, it was only logical, Ken thought, that we would go to him, so he wouldn't have to go to Rick. For some time, we were at the bottom of the bartender's list of priorities, because we were there for his personal benefit and he first had to keep his customers happy. While we waited for his attention, I broke into his routine long enough to ask where the ladies' room was. After pointing in the direction of my mission, he said, "There's no lock on the door. Someone will be there in a minute to watch the door for you."

So off I went. I did what I needed to do and returned to the bar, where Ken was still waiting for the bartender's attention. About five minutes later, a friendly young man walked up to us at the bar and asked, "Are you the lady who needs someone to watch the door?"

The fifth of February was Rick's birthday, three days before mine. We developed a kinship about that so we could celebrate our birthdays together. Rick was a fan of Gore Vidal, and I knew that he had read *1876*, so I bought him a copy of Gore Vidal's *Lincoln*, inscribed it with a suitable message concerning the future of our mutually observed birthdays, and presented it to him. All too soon, before he had a chance to begin reading it, he was in the hospital fighting pneumonia. Incessant coughing wore him down and made it difficult for him to develop an appetite—but not too difficult for an occasional smoke. Most days, he would save his desserts for me and they were adding up, both on his tray table and on my hips. Some days, if I happened to be visiting when the meal wagon arrived, he would suggest that I eat his dinner, because he wasn't going to anyway. On one of these occasions, it became an embarrassment to me when the nurse arrived to pick up the meal tray and, noticing that all of the food had been consumed, told Rick how proud she was of him for finishing the entire meal. Rick didn't see the point in confessing the truth, as he didn't think he would be leaving the hospital alive. My chastising him for smoking as the worst thing he could do for his health was met with, "It's the only pleasure I have left in my life."

Once again, things were put in perspective for me. And he *didn't* leave the hospital alive.

1985

18.
Brief Encounters

During that summer of 1985, the foundation asked me, as an advocate, to do an intake for a man who claimed to be positive that he had pneumocystis carnii pneumonia (PCP). I called him to set a time for our meeting. He asked if I would be driving a car identifying the AIDS Foundation. I assured him that I was driving my own personal vehicle. That wasn't enough for him. He wanted to be certain that the car didn't have a magnetic sign on both sides. Again, I assured him that wasn't the case. The point was that he didn't want his neighbors to see anything that might identify him as a possible candidate for the virus. I understood that to mean that he didn't want them to think he was gay; he didn't live in the right neighborhood for that.

I wrote down the information he provided, but he never explained what he wanted from the foundation. I think he wanted me to determine whether or not he was HIV-positive, but mainly, he wanted to talk. He confided that he had participated in some "dumb" activity and now he was scared. He wanted my home telephone number, which was not to be given, but I convinced him to get tested. The following week, I called him to follow through with my assignment, and he told me that he tested negative. I have not heard of him since.

***

Don was too sick to call for help. His previous lover contacted the foundation for help with a will. When I arrived at his home, the ex-lover answered the door and ushered me into the living room, where Don was lying on the couch. He had become totally blind from cytomegalovirus, the same infection Bob, our second client, had contracted. He was so thin and his body so twisted that he resembled the worst-looking victims of the Holocaust. To make matters worse, he was suffering from a severe case of dementia. He insisted, in his garbled voice, that he was able to drive his car, which made it even more obvious that something was wrong with his mind. Besides being unable to see, he couldn't even sit up by himself, much less drive a car. In order to spare a smidgen of his dignity, I allowed him, over the objections of his friend, to sign his own intake form, even though his oversized childlike scrawl trailed about the page. No one at the Social Services Committee meeting the following Monday night said a word about it. His application for assistance was accepted.

***

That autumn, the AIDS Foundation called me one afternoon to give me an assignment. I was to visit a small farmhouse out in the countryside west of where I lived. It was early evening when I headed out of town. As the sun was setting ahead of me, I finally reached the dusty, narrow lane where I was to turn in. After driving a short distance, I was greeted by not only the sound of barking dogs, but also their personal appearance at the bumper and door of my car. Other animals joined them, including chickens and goats. Apprehensively, I forced my way through the menagerie and made it to the front door of the house. The PWA wasn't there, but that didn't matter. His former lover, together with a new partner, was caring for him at home and they were in need of financial assistance for their friend. There were two older gentlemen there who had been together for many, many years. It was obvious that they were all concerned about the person with AIDS. It was the first time I had witnessed the overlapping of partners, in which a newcomer was more than willing to help out his current lover's previous companion. It would not be the last time I witnessed this phenomenon. More and more, it was becoming obvious that the gay population was forming closer and tighter bonds within their ranks. I was proud to be a part of the caring well.

***

During the first year of my enthusiastic participation in doing *mitzvahs* (Hebrew for good deeds), the foundation asked me to make an appointment with Harmon, a man who had been diagnosed as HIV-positive and simply wanted some information about the virus. At the time, I happened to be reading a book on the subject and offered to give it to him. Harmon asked me if it had a plain brown wrapper. I believe I understood why he asked, but it was an unusual coincidence that I was able to answer yes. I don't know why I had covered it, but it was instantly ready to be delivered to him. I was having lunch with Truman the day I had arranged to visit Harmon and take the book to him. Truman was happy to accompany me to Harmon's apartment, and it relieved my self-imposed tension about meeting, once again, someone who was new to the club. We were very well received, so I was delighted when Harmon called me the next week to go with him to an outdoor concert. He drove his almost antique Mercedes convertible to the park and left it in the parking lot with the top down. When I questioned that decision, he replied, "It's better than having the top slashed. If someone wants something, they'll find a way to get it."

It was obvious he had had prior experiences with that. When we returned to the car after the concert, sure enough, it had been vandalized—but the only thing missing was a comb.

The next time I saw Harmon, he was in the VA Hospital for treatment of dementia. He expressed concern as to whether or not he was "cogent." I thought to myself, if he's using a word like that to describe what he's afraid of, he can't possibly be demented.

I feel bad that I don't remember why our connection dissipated, but I know he died shortly thereafter.

1985

19.
Tony

Since by this time the team was functioning as a loosely knit band of helpers, we each encountered someone somewhere who needed something. Ken and I made rounds, performing miscellaneous favors around town. We lost track of Cecil and Chris, but Steve, having joined the Buddy Team, the new one-on-one care service, was still acting in that capacity for whomever was assigned to him by the foundation. Steve and I still saw each other frequently and talked endlessly on the phone, even though our once common ground shifted to a different level. Although Ken and I were no longer working as members of a team, which had once included Steve, I was mostly involved with Ken, our elected team captain, because he made it so—whether it was in the capacity of AIDS Foundation assignments or to assist personal friends who requested our help.

On one occasion, Tony, a very close friend of Ken's, was in need of a notary public to witness and sign "Do Not Resuscitate" documents. I had met Tony before and had seen him around the neighborhood, in restaurants and occasionally a gay bar when I was out with Ken or Truman, or both. Making good use of my notary privileges, which had been paid for by Richard, my employer and Bob's stair rail builder, Ken drove me to see Tony to ensure that his legal papers were signed.

Tony was confined to the apartment he shared with two

friends, Michael K. and Jay, and at that time was completely dependent upon others to keep him alive. There were so many people in that interim stage between life and death, with nothing that hospitalization could do for them; so friends relied on each other for their last-stage support.

As I entered Tony's room, where he lay awaiting my arrival, I was astounded by how much he had changed since the last time I had seen him. He had lost so much weight he was almost unrecognizable. Before we got around to the formalities that brought me to his bedside, Tony asked me, "Did you see my legs?"

I wasn't sure why he asked, so I tried to ignore the question. He repeated it, so I replied, "No I didn't, but I don't need to."

It was Tony's turn to ignore my comment. He motioned to Ken to raise the thin sheet that covered his frail body. What I saw was a totally nude man with deep purple skin from the top of his feet all the way up to his waist. He was completely covered with the ravages of Kaposi's sarcoma. It was never explained to me why he wanted me to see that, but it caused me to feel incredibly sorry for what Tony had endured, and added another unforgettable image to my dubious collection of AIDS information.

After explaining to Tony what the DNR document meant, I asked him, more than once, if he understood its contents, and if he was certain that he wanted to execute it. I clarified that the decision was his own. He assured me that he was positive on all three points. But even though my questions were redundant, I felt, for Tony's sake and mine, that I had to ask them. I was experiencing a sense of power with which I did not feel comfortable. The next day, Ken—ever the bearer of bad tidings—called to tell me that Tony was gone.

1985

20.
Novelette

Michigan was my home for most of my life before moving south. In the middle of July, in the big city where AIDS had gotten a firm grip by the middle of 1985, I wasn't too keen on having to leave home, where air-conditioners hummed in every window. Summers were miserably hot. But my commitment was solid, and when I received a request to visit the family of a young black woman with AIDS, I heeded the call. I wasn't sure what they needed or wanted from the AIDS Foundation, and I'm not sure they did, either.

In the hot, stuffy, not air-conditioned house were Novelette's sister, Diane (the one who called for assistance), her mother, and an assortment of small children. It was difficult to determine which children were Novelette's and which were her sister's, but that didn't matter. I began by asking how they had found out about the AIDS Foundation. One of the children was told to find her mother's purse, from which was drawn a small scrap of paper with three capital letters written on it: KFA, along with the phone number of the AIDS Foundation. At the time, the organization was named KS/AIDS Foundation, so they probably misheard the name as KFA. They didn't tell me where they had gotten that information, but it was what they needed and they used it to reach out for help.

They told me that Novelette was in the hospital, so

whatever had been the reason for their call, it was put on hold for the time being. I don't know why I told them that most of the clients we had were gay men, and that if they were to become involved with the organization or any of its social services, they should be apprised of that, in case they had a problem with it. They assured me they didn't. That, too, would soon become irrelevant.

There wasn't much else to do that day, since Novelette wasn't there and no one had much more to say to me. However, as they spoke among themselves, there was a lot of cross talk, but I couldn't understand their jargon and tried to find a graceful way of exiting. I left with a very uncomfortable feeling that I had once again crossed over from gay turf, where I was quite at home, to a new and different demographic zone. It was becoming apparent that AIDS had infiltrated the straight black community in some way with which I was not yet familiar.

The following week, I made a courtesy phone call to the house to ask how Novelette was progressing. I offered to go to the county hospital to meet her and they quickly agreed. Her sister and mother, sans children, were there when I arrived.

Diane and her mother introduced me to a young, unresponsive woman who occupied the bed, in a stark setting very unlike the ones in the hospitals where insurance was the magic word for the quality of care afforded the patients. Novelette's mother wanted her to know that help, such as it was, had arrived, and she kept insisting that Novelette acknowledge my presence.

"Novelette, it's Mama. There's someone here to see you. Say hello." It was apparent to me that there would be no reply.

I had seen television coverage of some of the worst AIDS cases, which showed yellowed eyes bulging in their sockets, skin covered with bumps of unknown origin, and all manner of afflictions. This was what Novelette was dealing with, but I'm not sure she was aware of it. She was blind and in a pathetic stage of dementia, where no amount of prodding could bring her into the circle of conversation that surrounded her.

Novelette's lunch was presented on a dark brown tray: a cold, unappetizing hamburger on a bun, potato chips, and a drink. The nurse had set it aside, as if she knew—as well as the rest of us—that it would not be eaten. It was a given that meals were delivered, but they were hardly ever consumed by the people with AIDS whom I had met. First of all, the food was never tasty, and the appetite would have had to be very healthy to even consider eating it.

We weren't getting anywhere and neither was Novelette. It was only a matter of days before I received a call that she had died. Since I had not done much to help the family, and never really found out what they might have needed, I felt that I should at least attend Novelette's funeral. The AIDS Foundation had no protocol about whether volunteers should or should not go. August 17, a hot and sultry Saturday, found the Pleasant Grove Missionary Baptist Church filled with people who had come to pay their respects. I took a seat on the aisle near the back of the sanctuary, after having nervously walked up the center aisle to where the casket was placed at the foot of the altar. I was rather surprised to find Novelette's body in an open casket, but even more surprised that she did not in the least resemble the person I had seen at the hospital. Embalming, makeup, and a wig had completely changed her appearance.

The service began with a long procession of family members walking slowly in single file, except for Diane and her mother, who walked arm in arm. Behind them was one of the pretty little girls I had met at the house just a few short weeks before.

As they passed my row, the child tapped her grandmother's shoulder and, having gotten her attention, pointed to me to let her grandmother know I was there. I was exceedingly grateful for that gesture. They proceeded to the front row, sat down, and waited for the pastor to begin.

I had never before been to a church where the entire congregation was black, so I was completely unprepared for the style of funeral service being held for Novelette. Before the pastor had completed his opening remarks, an assortment of men on the altar began chanting "amen," and throughout the service, no matter what the pastor said, the amens followed. Novelette was not honored, nor did her passing seem to grieve him. Instead, he warned the assembly that if we led our lives in the manner of the deceased, we were doomed to her punishment: early death and damnation.

"If you live the kind of life as Sister Novelette, you'll end up like her," he shouted, pointing to the open casket in which Novelette lay, fortunately not aware of the manner in which Brother Jackson was sending her to her eternal reward.

I was appalled at what I heard, until I realized that Novelette's family was joining in with amens of their own. I was relieved to realize that I was probably the only one in the congregation who was hearing this kind of litany for the first time, and that it was the acceptable norm for them.

But as the pastor went on, he spoke of his own upbringing and the exemplary manner in which he had risen from poverty and hardship to where he was today. It was like no funeral service I had ever attended, in which someone other than the deceased had been lauded for their service to mankind. I had to settle for believing that the family was satisfied with the service.

The family retreated from the front of the church in

reverse order from which they had entered. When Diane and her mother reached my row, they stopped to hug me and thank me for attending the funeral service. In spite of my original discomfort, which had dissipated when the little girl saw me, I was also very glad that I had gone.

Outside the church, as family and friends gathered to offer their condolences once again, Novelette's brother invited me to the reception being held at his home. After thanking the family for including me in their plans, I explained that I would have liked to attend, but was scheduled to make a hospital visit that afternoon.

1985

21.
Same Day—Different Mission

My sister-in-law had just been diagnosed with cancer of the stomach and I was on my way to the hospital to visit her. I hadn't seen her in two years because of a family rift about Gary's diagnosis. I wouldn't realize for many years that there were other families who rejected one of their own who had been diagnosed with AIDS. In fact, it was not uncommon, but I surely hadn't expected it from my family. The day that Gary had called me to inform me of his diagnosis, I was to have had lunch with one of my three brothers. When he arrived at my office to meet me, I told him of Gary's call. He confirmed with me that it was something that affected only gay men—which, at the time, we took to be so—and he told me that it would not be discussed when I visited his home and family. They would be told that Gary had cancer. It took me only seconds to make the decision to no longer go to his home. That night, I received a call from my brother's wife, asking what they could do to help me. I answered, "Just accept me, however I am." I had hoped I would hear from them, but didn't, until my sister-in-law's diagnosis.

As I entered her room, seeing her asleep, I was reminded of Novelette. And yet, here was a different person; still alive, but probably not for very much longer. I don't know if my sister-in-law had been amenable to my exile, but she didn't seem to object to my visit. Her first words when she opened her eyes and saw me in the room were, "How is Gary?"

She could have just been asking in general; after all, we hadn't spoken in over two years. But I took her question to be specific.

"I didn't know you knew about his illness," I told her.

She replied, "Of course I knew. Why did we have to hear about Rock Hudson before anybody would acknowledge AIDS?"

So much for that. Two years of our relationship had been lost. When I was leaving the hospital with one of my nieces, I asked if the family had known of Gary's illness. She told me, "Sure we did. We just didn't talk about it."

Three months later, my sister-in-law passed away. Gary and I had lost someone who was very dear to us in spite of her absence from our lives. His condolence message to her family, cousins with whom he had grown up, read, "I remember her taste and creativity, her drive and devotion. Now I ponder her qualities magnified without physical bounds. Goodbye, bon voyage, Aunt B.R."

1985

22.
Bill

O n a Saturday morning, less than two weeks after my sister-in-law died on November 5, I received a call from the AIDS Foundation, asking me to call Bill's parents, Bill Sr. and Marge, who had come to Houston from Ohio. They called him Billy, although I knew him as Bill. He was in the intensive care unit and his parents had no one to turn to. I was given the phone number of Bill's apartment. Although I was accustomed to what had become a routine event, I certainly was not looking forward to it. Before I could make myself dial Bill's number, I had to give myself the usual pep talk: "Think of what these people are going through. They are new to the city, they don't know anyone except their son, and he is sick and may be dying."

Damn, I hated this.

The split second between hearing the phone ring and the sound of a woman's voice marked the beginning of an enduring friendship. The voice revealed the all too familiar tone of a mother's anxiety. From that moment, I felt reassured once again that I had done the right thing.

Bill's mother wasn't exactly frantic; she was simply at a loss. She and her husband had only a few days before been informed that they needed to go to their son's bedside. They had no idea what was coming next. That same afternoon, we met for the first time. As I stepped out of the elevator into the visitors' waiting area located between the elevators and the ICU, they rose to meet me. Of course, I was sure they were the couple I was looking for, but they could only guess that I was the AIDS Foundation advocate (whatever that meant to them). Their warm personalities, and the fact that they had come to town from the same Ohio city where I was born, immediately drew me to these people. That proved to be a very convenient icebreaker.

Because visiting time in the ICU was limited—two times per hour, ten minutes per visit, and two people only—we had a long time to get to know each other and to talk about Bill's illness. I didn't know how much they knew, so I tried to allow them to do most of the talking. I had arrived immediately after the 2:00 PM visitation, so when the time came for the next one, Bill's father insisted that I go in with Marge to be introduced. She had warned me that Bill would probably be very disagreeable and cranky. That concerned me until I recalled that he, or his representative, was required to have requested that an advocate be sent to see what he needed. Therefore, I assumed he would welcome my visit. Whatever his attitude, I resolved to maintain my composure, knowing that I could at least handle this initial visit. Besides, all I had to do was get in, do the intake, and get out. Right!

Billy was hooked up to a ventilator, with the familiar blue tubes fed into his throat. His eyes told me he was glad I was there. What a relief that was. He reached for the traditional pad and pencil reserved for these occasions, and hastily scribbled notes to let me know what he needed. He didn't want money or a place to live. He wanted someone to help his parents get through the ordeal. At that time, the limited number of female volunteers—particularly mothers—meant I was *it*. In fact, that was what the caller from the AIDS Foundation had told me that morning. Bill was quite able to fill in the required forms, and by the time he completed that task our ten minutes had elapsed. In the small foyer outside of Billy's room was a lavatory where visitors were required to wash their hands before leaving the area. Once again, as in the ICU where Arthur, our first client, had been at a different hospital, it seemed silly to me to reverse the sequence of protective measures. They were the ones with no immune system!

As I left Billy's room, I could tell that we were all in it together for the long haul. I couldn't bear to leave Billy's parents by themselves, especially since they had nothing to do but wait forty minutes of every hour to see their son for ten short minutes. After what seemed like an interminable wait, it was Billy's dad's turn to see him. The two mothers stayed behind. When he returned, Bill Sr. announced that he had had a "talk" with Billy, combining the son's note writing and his father's speaking.

"Billy told me he had something to tell me. He said, 'Dad, I have AIDS.' Then he says, 'Dad, I have something else to tell you. I'm gay.' So I says, 'So what? You're our son. You're sick and we love you and we're here to help you.'"

I was dumbstruck. This man was wonderful! So many of the gay people I had come to know were terrified of having their parents know they were gay. And it certainly wasn't uncommon for parents to find this out simultaneously with learning that their child had AIDS. I had pleaded with so many so often to tell their parents one or both pieces of information, whichever applied, because they could either confirm their worst fears and know what they were dealing with, or find that they had lost a lot of time staying away from parents who loved them unconditionally.

The partner of one my dearest and closest friends was

HIV-positive and chose to keep his status hidden from everyone. Only when he contracted PCP did my friend learn the news, but he was forbidden to tell anyone. That included family, friends, acquaintances, *anyone*! But my friend revealed it to me because he desperately needed someone to talk with. He noticed that I wore a red ribbon, which was a symbol of support for people infected or affected by HIV/AIDS. After I had gotten to know his partner, I tried to encourage the man to tell his family, but was met with a steadfast refusal to do so because he didn't want to upset them.

I asked him, "Do you believe it would not upset them more to find out if and when you become ill?"

He held his ground, all the way to the day he entered the hospital a year later. He died from lymphoma of the brain. His whole family came to be with him, praying feverishly at his bedside and encouraging him to fight for his life. But none of that saved him, and his mother couldn't seem to understand his rationale.

"Why couldn't he tell me? I'm his mother."

A few years went by, and a long-distance phone call came from her. She repeated the same words, "Why couldn't he tell me? I'm his mother."

My personal opinion was that people who chose that approach weren't giving themselves or their parents an opportunity to spend valuable time together, whether they were sick or not. Their family may have wanted to help them through their illness, as Bill's had. Because of their devotion to their son, I knew for sure that I liked these people.

I invited Billy's parents to lunch at the same restaurant where Ken's car used to find its own way. Billy gave us a thumbs-up on the choice. It had become the easiest decision when selecting an eating and meeting place. Very often, family members would treat the caregivers to a meal, to express their gratitude for our help.

When we returned to the hospital, the first two of the three of us to visit Bill were his mother and I. Now I was becoming more comfortable with him, having at least been welcomed as someone who would relieve some measure of pressure from his parents. They had an ally and someone to call on and relate to.

On Thanksgiving Day, I couldn't stop thinking about Billy and his parents. Yet, I did what I always do on Thanksgiving. I made the usual sweet potato casserole and spent the holiday at the home of my brother, Elliot, and his family. My thoughts of what I could have done or should have done wouldn't leave me. I wasn't sure what those things would have been, but I knew I was leaving somebody out. The next day, upon arriving at the hospital, my thoughts were confirmed. Billy wasn't concerned for himself, but he felt very bad for his parents, who were so extremely saddened by having spent a traditional family holiday in a strange city. Not only did they not have the comfort of their other children and relatives, but they didn't even know where they could go to have a decent meal. My feelings of guilt mounted, but we all got through the day. It didn't seem like it at the time, but there were more important things in store.

After Billy's PCP had responded to treatment, the ventilator was removed, and he was transferred to a private room. By then his parents had to return home; they were comfortable at his apartment, but knew no one in town besides me and they were getting anxious.

Billy's medication nauseated him more than once. Upon my entering his room one day, he cautioned me on how to get to his bedside without stepping in the tuna salad vomit he had deposited on the floor. For as long as I can remember, one of my greatest aversions has been to witness someone in the throes of vomiting—or, for that matter, seeing the results of it. This day was my true test for steadfastly adhering to my commitment to help people with AIDS. If I couldn't accept the inevitability of nausea, I knew I'd better find something else to do.

The oxygen administered to Bill came from a tank that was attached to an outlet in the wall, but he was eager to go for a walk around the circular pod of the AIDS unit.

"Unplug the oxygen," he instructed me.

"Are you serious?" I asked. I thought he would die if I did.

"Yes! Pull the plug"

I didn't like the sound of that. Pull the plug. We each repeated our words over and over until I was convinced that "pulling the plug" did not have the connotation I had for so long understood. I did as I was asked, helped Bill out of bed, and we were off—Bill with his IV pole while I pushed the wheeled oxygen tank alongside.

Until that time, Bill had been agitated and frustrated with his plight. I sensed that he had thoughts of giving up. But after the trip around the pod, on a subsequent visit I found him in such good spirits that I had to inquire what had happened to change his attitude. He had been encouraged by the hospital staff to attend the physical therapy sessions that were available in the hospital. Not only had it improved his health, but his outlook as well. What had excited him so was that he was enlisting other AIDS patients to join the group. Now he looked forward to going to the gym (as he called the physical therapy room) to work out, and until he left the hospital, his outlook was upbeat.

Once he returned to his apartment, we met for dinner

occasionally and spent time together talking about his family, his crocheting hobby, and mutual friends. Before his illness forced Bill into retiring on disability, he had worked as a waiter at a popular restaurant. We frequented it so he could visit with his former coworkers; besides, they gave him free meals. It offered him a sense of connectedness even though he no longer worked there. Other times, we picked up Chinese food and took it to his place. Once, when we were ready to indulge in egg rolls and fried rice, Bill realized he wasn't hungry after all and had to forego the meal. Of course, that was never a surprise to me, after having seen it happen often with some of the other PWAs I had known.

On a dreary Saturday afternoon in December, I received a call that Bill was back in the hospital. When I arrived in his room, he was surrounded by friends, some of them sitting on his bed with him. It looked as if he were holding court, with his loyal subjects doing his bidding. I was relieved to see that so many people had rallied to his support. Among them was one of Gary's closest friends, Tim. Not Joe's Tim—Tim who would come into my life in additional, significant ways. What a coincidence, although it was becoming more the norm to continually encounter people I knew. The AIDS community was not only closing in around us, it was getting closer within itself. It was 1985 and we had been waging this war for over two years. Why hadn't we won after all this time? The medical experts had said it would be five years before there would be a cure, but for God's sake, people were dying all around us. Why couldn't somebody do something to stop the suffering? Who knew it would be one five-year promise after another for many years to come?

Driving home from the hospital late that Saturday night, I fell into a strangely philosophical frame of mind, thinking about where we were all going from there. Bill, Tim, Gary, Ken, Truman—all of us who had become so inextricably connected. The network, which began when I encountered Gary, the first executive director of the AIDS Foundation, was expanding exponentially. As I met more and more people involved in the fight against AIDS, their lives began to intersect with each other's, or I would find myself running into friends or acquaintances who already knew each other before I became a link in their chain of destiny.

1985

23.
Finding Serenity

Something was beckoning me to calm down, to find not only a logical explanation but also a sense of peace. The car radio was on, but I wasn't really hearing it as I drove home after my visit with Billy and his friends. I changed stations, one after another; then, for the first time, I heard *Hearts of Space*. It seemed to be sending the most serene music across the airwaves from heaven. Over time, it would change my life. Arriving home, I rushed into the house to get an audiotape in place to record the rest of the program. I had to send this to Gary. I knew it would affect him as it had me, the same way we had reacted when seeing the opera *Salome*, and simultaneously nudged each other at the playing of a particularly beautiful chord. Having never before heard what was a regular, Saturday night, prerecorded program on our local public radio station, I soon learned that there was no advertising during the broadcast, and at the end of the hour, the announcer would give the playlist of the music on that evening's program. That night, the announcer and co-producer was Anna Turner. Her voice transported me to another dimension. I felt as though I were floating through a dream sequence that brought peace to my heart and soul. My mind immediately placed a face to the voice of Anna Turner, and I was hooked. The timing was impeccable. After the names of the pieces of music and their composers were given, Anna gave the address to which her audience could write for additional information. The city was San Francisco. How perfectly serendipitous! Gary's city! I should have known. It was, for me, the magical coming together of what was right about the whole world, and why I was in it.

Of course, the next day I had to tell Gary of my transition from anxiety to peace, from chaos to calm. As it turned out, he was a faithful listener of the same program and understood my feelings. The following week, realizing that I would soon be in San Francisco for my annual Christmas week holiday visit with Gary, I wrote to the producers of *Hearts of Space* to ask if I could meet them, using my involvement with AIDS and their being in San Francisco (a rather flimsy connection) as my entrée. The reply from Stephen Hill was written on a beautiful picture postcard showing the top of the Golden Gate Bridge shrouded in very dense fog. He explained that they did not usually honor such requests, but made an exception for me. I was deeply touched, but very nervous and apprehensive about the coming meeting. I had placed them on a tall pedestal in a fantasyland of bright, twinkling stars against the crisp, cold, clear night sky of San Francisco. In my mind, they were the angels of serenity.

I had to make the trip to their studio through the city by myself, so I drove past the building the day before my official visit, in order to find my way and to avoid arriving late the next day. It was in a rather run-down part of San Francisco, but as far as I was concerned, it was Shangri-la. The bumper sticker on Anna's little Nissan, parked outside of the building, read "Reach for the Stars." It was magic to me, just as every single thing I did in San Francisco—especially with my son—was magic.

It was shortly before this time that Gary and his lover, Gary C., had ended their relationship. They had both worked for the same oil company for five years, and when the firm's headquarters were moved to Alaska, both were offered the opportunity to go. Gary C. chose the move; my Gary did not. He sought another job, and had no trouble finding the position he held at Lawrence Berkeley Laboratories for the rest of his life.

We had previously spent much of the holiday week with Gary C. This time, Gary was home from work for the holidays and had been cutting and fitting sheet metal for the furnace vents in his bedroom. It was part of his ongoing home remodeling project.

Bidding goodbye to Gary the day after my trial run, I nervously drove to the radio station to meet my angels. Anna, who looked very much as I had envisioned her, was eating lunch, and Stephen Hill[1], the producer, showed me around the studio. We exchanged pleasantries and I took a few snapshots of them. I mentioned that the music they played sounded, to me, like "music to die by," and immediately felt foolish for having said that. But Stephen assured me that it was very real to them and others in the Bay Area. He told me of an occasion when a doctor had taken an audiotape of a symphony written by Bay Area composer Constance Demby[2] to the AIDS wing of the hospital, to help soothe a critically ill patient of his. The following testimonial was written to Ms. Demby, who has graciously given her permission for it to be included here.

As my AIDS patient lay dying, Novus Magnificat filled the halls of the hospital. He was hooked up to machines that showed his life signs, and when he flat-lined and passed over with the very last note of the symphony, we knew he and the music had become one. He timed it perfectly for his passing over. The halls were filled with doctors, nurses and patients either weeping or wondering what was happening.

P. Debarone, D.D.

In 1988, when Stephen Hill was in Houston to participate in our public radio fund-raising drive, I was a very active volunteer at the station. Immediately upon my entering the studio, Stephen greeted me by asking, "How is Gary?"

He had not known that I would be at the station, and I had not expected him to remember me, so I was very touched that when he saw me, he asked about Gary. A few days before, I had had one of the photos I had taken of him at his studio in San Francisco enlarged and had posted it on the bulletin board at our radio station. Taking him by surprise, and knowing that he hadn't furnished it to the station, he asked, "Where did that come from?"

I guess I should have given it to him.

1985

(1)   I have remained in touch with Stephen over the years, calling him when I was in San Francisco, and later by email. He has informed me that Anna Turner died of pancreatic cancer in 1996. To learn more about *Hearts of Space* and Stephen Hill, log on to www.hos.com. The program has been developed as an online service, where all previous programs can be heard for a small fee. The weekly radio program is free.

(2)   Constance Demby is a composer of meditative and sacred space music. For more information about her background, music, recordings, and testimonials, go to www.constancedemby.com

24.
Jan

On a warm, sunny day in February, I was assigned to drive far across the city to do an intake, in order to learn the precise needs of the client. That particular day caused me to rethink the magnitude of the crisis.

The door to the lovely home was opened by a beautiful young woman of twenty-five. She had blonde hair and blue eyes, and was impeccably groomed and well dressed. She gave me a tour of the large house, which was immaculately clean, well organized, and obviously the pride of its inhabitant. But as she began telling me her story, I began to realize that this was not a happy home.

Jan had been married, and the young couple had expected their first child two years before. When a miscarriage ended the pregnancy, Jan required a blood transfusion. As no one knew what was lurking in the hospital's blood supplies, Jan became an unfortunate recipient of infected blood. In the subsequent months, she began to feel the ill effects of the infection and consulted one doctor after another. None had the knowledge to ascertain what might have happened to her. Sure, they knew about AIDS, but they weren't looking for it in the likes of Jan.

She had a good job, where she was responsible for signing company checks, bookkeeping, and numerous other valuable tasks. However, her absenteeism was growing, and her employer and coworkers didn't believe the seemingly continuous complaints of her ill health. After all, she looked great. Meanwhile, her condition deteriorated until one physician, after exhausting all other possibilities, tested her for the HIV virus—and the mystery was solved. But her problems only continued to get worse. Her husband, who had been very supportive, vowed to stay with her and take care of her "to the end," but as time passed, more of him was roving than his eye. They eventually divorced, leaving Jan to fend for herself. She apparently was coping fairly well until she made the decision to inform her employer of her diagnosis. Then the pressures at work increased further, by her removal from the company checking account and her relegation to a back room to prevent her from possibly infecting others. These added insults finally drove her to resign from her job. As I listened to Jan's story, I was overwhelmed with anger. I was frustrated enough with the discrimination I had heard about from the gay men, but this was my first experience with AIDS in the heterosexual population. My empathy for Jan as a disenfranchised working woman was another issue that gnawed at my sense of justice. But at the moment, that wasn't the problem. My volunteerism had just taken a different tack, as I entered the world of universal AIDS discrimination. Gay, straight; it was irrelevant. What the world wasn't heeding was that anyone, *gay* or *straight*, could pass along what had come to be known as the gift that keeps on giving. And they weren't talking about the United Way. What it meant, exponentially speaking and in the context of AIDS, was that when a person had sex, they were having sex with everyone with whom their partner had had sex, and so on, and so on. The spread of HIV/AIDS was inevitable. This was the enormity of the pandemic.

Arriving home, I realized I had spent five very intense

hours with Jan. I called her to find out how she felt about our meeting and we talked for another hour. After I hung up the phone, I cried uncontrollably.

Jan had called the AIDS Foundation because she wanted a buddy. She didn't request financial or food assistance, housing, or taxi vouchers. She just wanted a friend. I told her about the AIDS Foundation support group, which met on Monday nights in the church fellowship hall; the church where so many of the gay men were members; where I had met Steve at one of the early meetings of the foundation before it had a place to call its own.

The following Monday night, after I had seen my therapist, Gary T., I also met with Jim, the current president of the AIDS Foundation. Before my Advocate Team meeting, I dropped in on the support group to see if Jan had made the long trip from her home to attend. Arriving after they had begun, and trying to enter quietly without disturbing the meeting in progress, I was greeted by Jan's interruption of the speaker and her smiling voice announcing to the group, "This is my new buddy."

It took me my surprise. I couldn't be her buddy. If I had assumed that role in Jan's life, I would have had to discontinue my work as an advocate. We were only supposed to get the information, turn it in, and disconnect. And we could only function in one role at a time. Right then, I needed the advocacy job because I had previously gotten so close to the clients who had come before Jan that I was drained of the ability to cope with the loss of such intimate relationships. This would not be the first time I had to deal with that dilemma, and usually, I was not successful.

I never spoke with Jan again. I believe she moved to Dallas.

1986

25.
Jim

One of the volunteers from my second training session, with whom I had become quite close, had an uncanny amount of ESP. He told me of many incidents he had predicted which had come true; sometimes by circuitous routes, sometimes distressingly direct. He was a client of Jim, the president of the AIDS Foundation, who was also a therapist at the counseling center.

Monday, one week after I had had my meeting with Jim in his office, I was to attend a Social Services Committee meeting, where the advocates pleaded their cases on behalf of the people for whom they had done intakes the previous week. That day was my psychic friend's birthday, and when I phoned to greet him on his special day, he did not welcome the intended good wishes. He explained that he was highly agitated, but could not reveal the reason. After much cajoling and pleading with him to confide in me, he told me that he had an eerie feeling that something was wrong with Jim.

I said, "How can that be? I just saw him a week ago and he was fine."

Our committee meetings were held at the counseling center where Jim's office happened to be, in the same building where our weekend training sessions had been held. My friend was extremely upset, and could not begin to tell me what his underlying concern was. He simply said, "It's so bad I can't tell you what is wrong, but there will be a sign at your meeting tonight."

There was no bulletin board, so I assumed he meant that there would be inkling, an omen, nothing tangible. But there it was, a small *handwritten* note tacked to the wall in the waiting room. "Jim will not be seeing clients this week due to influenza."

I was stunned. There was, indeed, a sign. What on earth was going on? By the end of that week, Jim's health had taken a devastating turn for the worse.

My friend, of course, cursed his premonition. What he couldn't tell me before was that he had wanted to warn Jim to take care of himself, because he had a very strong feeling that something horrible was going to happen to him. And he feared that Jim would assume it was just another one of the coincidences his client had confided to him in the past, so he decided not to say anything. How could Jim have taken it seriously? Perhaps he hadn't placed much importance on his client's previous claims of ESP, so why start now?

It was learned that Jim had turned his healthcare over to two of the licensed therapists and two interns from the counseling center where he worked. The plan was to use what they called a rebirthing process to bring Jim back to health. Leading other HIV-infected people in how to deal with their illness, this method of treatment was simply not acceptable to the community. Jim and the therapists refused to allow his parents to visit with him. He had the right to decide not to tell his parents of his condition or of his chosen method of treatment, but the fact remained that Jim, as president of the AIDS Foundation, and the therapists, whose client base included many people with HIV/AIDS, had used a treatment course outside of the accepted practice of the center and the

AIDS Foundation. It was decided to remove his life support at 6:00 PM the following Monday.

Jim's funeral was a beautiful tribute to a man who had led his troops from the counseling center and the AIDS Foundation. Musical performances from professional opera singers, bagpipers, and the organist of the Methodist church where the service was held offered comfort to the mourners, but I'm not certain that many of them knew what had transpired the previous week.

I never even knew that Jim had been living with AIDS.

1986

26.
The Third Michael

Michael K., who had been the go-between for Tony's notary needs, became the next object of our attention. He was a friend of Ken's, who had introduced us the night I had notarized Tony's DNR directive. Tony was living at Michael's apartment at the time.

Michael was a man of musical talent and good looks, who also had exquisite taste in home furnishings. He had been married and divorced, and had a teenage daughter who lived in another city. He was at the stage of his illness where there was no available protocol to add a measure of comfort to his remaining days. Ken and I had had dinner on occasion with Michael, and I enjoyed his company very much because I also had a musical background. I didn't really know Michael very well, nor did I have very much time to change that. Before long, he was being cared for by a rotation of visiting nurses. I don't recall doing anything particularly meritorious for him, besides getting him a new watchband when he was no longer able to leave the house, but something must have inspired him. One day, not long after that simple act was done, I was sitting at my desk at work when a floral delivery person arrived with a beautiful arrangement of a dozen white roses. Having accustomed myself to observing similar deliveries for several single young ladies in our office, I was pleasantly surprised to learn that it was for me. The accompanying card read, "What a wonderful world this would be if everyone in it was as sweet as you. Love, Michael." I don't mention that here to boast of my great deed, only to relate how much mileage I got from my coworkers by receiving flowers and a loving message from an appreciative gentleman. They didn't need to know the circumstances.

1986

27.
Harry

In Michael's final days, his friend Harry called on him often, not only to keep him company, but also to perform any little task that Michael was unable to do. Harry had *it* too, and therefore could not work. Michael insisted on paying Harry to massage his feet, and Harry needed the money so he didn't refuse it. This was how I continued to find and lose new friends, overlapping one relationship with another. When Michael died, Ken asked me if I would drive Harry to the funeral. Having done so, we naturally sat together. As the service progressed, Harry fumbled around in his trouser pockets and fished out a well-used tissue. Upon noticing, I quickly gave him a fresh supply. He cried uncontrollably and blew his nose until the service was over, but not before confiding in me that he was in part crying for Michael, but also because, he said, "I'm probably going to be next."

After the church service for Michael, some of our group went to a cafeteria for a midafternoon snack. Harry couldn't eat anything that had to be chewed or was spicy because of the Kaposi's sarcoma lesions in his throat. He ordered macaroni and cheese, and strawberry flavored Jell-O. After sampling one bite of each, he had to give up trying to eat. The following day, I prepared for him bland potato soup, with no salt or other seasoning. Along with that I pureed cantaloupe in the blender, thinking the juice would be mild enough for him to swallow.

At the first taste of the soup, it seemed to me that Harry's tall, thin body catapulted across the room, as I saw him smack against the opposite wall of the kitchen. Apparently, the soup irritated his sensitive throat, causing the involuntarily violent reaction. Unfortunately, the cantaloupe juice wasn't successful, either. From then on, it was touch and go for Harry when it came to food. I took him out for a picnic one day, just the two of us, and he seemed delighted to be outdoors, even if it was unbearably hot on that humid August day. Still, the only thing he enjoyed of the picnic was his root beer. He could no longer swallow solid food.

The following week, I called Harry from work at about 10:00 AM, just to check in and see how he was feeling. He said that he didn't feel very well, but didn't want to bother the doctor because, he said, "He's probably too busy with other patients."

Harry wasn't putting himself down; he was raising other people up. I insisted that I would make the call for him and he reluctantly agreed. It surprised me that the doctor returned my call so quickly, as he worked at two different county hospitals, and not only had an overload of patients, but had to go back and forth between the overcrowded facilities. He was the same physician who, in the early days of the KS Committee, was dumbfounded by the new illnesses that were showing up on his hospital's doorstep. I was instructed to immediately take Harry to what the doctor called the triage, at the hospital nearest his apartment, which was conveniently near my office. The rush hardly seemed to make a difference, because when we arrived at the pulmonary clinic, it was clear that our haste became a matter of "hurry up and wait." Patients were hustled into the system as if they were on a conveyor belt; yet once they were put on the "belt," the services they were provided were slow in coming. Time in the ER stretched into a lengthy wait for us, as other people who had arrived before us were sent off to their appointments. Harry's name was finally called and he, knowing how the system worked, presented his permanent plastic ID card and took his position in the line to be x-rayed. That was my first experience with the intricacies of a public hospital, and I was both impressed and disillusioned by the way it functioned. The fact that the professional staff showed up for work was what impressed me. It had to be a thankless job. My disillusionment came from the process taking so long; I was fearful that people would die during their encampment in the triage. They weren't separated into categories of urgency, which I felt would have been more efficient. Pregnant women arrived at the triage for their routine prenatal care, along with others of every other medical condition. It could have been better organized, but at least they weren't segregating the HIV cases from everyone else. That could have been for one of two reasons. They were either not as afraid of the virus as was the general population, or they didn't have the funds to provide separate services for them. I would not even begin to speculate which option was in effect. Efficiency didn't appear to be a priority in the county-run institution, but it offered job security for the staff. There was a never-ending procession of county citizens utilizing the facility.

We finally were given instructions to take Harry's records and previous x-rays to the radiology department, to have some new chest pictures taken. I was pushing the wheelchair, but Harry's energy exceeded mine. He would sort of leap forward from the chair to press elevator buttons. If his problem hadn't been so dire, it might have felt like we were having fun.

A local church, other than the one where the support group was held, had finally come around to becoming involved with AIDS. One of their care team members was assigned to help Harry. I had been told by Harry of the many things Dottie had done for him, for which he was grateful. But during his wheelchair ride through the hospital corridors, he told me that he was upset when Dottie insisted that he go with her to the Baptist church, of which *she* was a member.

"I kept trying to tell her that I am a Methodist. Why can't she understand that? Sometimes I just feel like throwing her against the wall!"

To my recollection, Dottie dropped out of the picture for the next few weeks.

We spent the next few hours in various laboratories, ending with the taking of blood gas levels. Harry was very apprehensive of this procedure, having endured it before. He described it as feeling as if a screwdriver were being driven up the vein in his wrist. He couldn't see me crying, as he was lying prone on a table around the corner of the wall where I was sitting. I glanced to my right to see only his head extending beyond the corner, his face contorted into a grimace as they rammed the invasive tool into his arm.

By the time Harry had gone through the multitude of medical assaults to his sore and now tired body, he was admitted to the hospital. Thinking about it after twenty-one years, I don't recall that anyone had told me what his diagnosis was. I was so used to being with the young warriors, in or out of the hospital, it must not have made a difference to me why he was admitted. He just was. I pushed the wheelchair (come to think of it, where was a nurse's aide?) to Harry's assigned room and waited while he changed into hospital pj's behind the curtain he had closed for privacy. When he stood on the bed to open the curtain, the mattress was unstable so I held onto Harry's waist. He let out a scream of pain, which I had caused by breaking the crust of a very large KS lesion. Blood ran down his side. It seemed to me as if everything I had done that day had lost its value, become null and void because of this major goof-up. Harry made it a much smaller problem for himself than it was for me, or maybe it was because he was familiar with the gentle art of savoir faire.

The morning all of these events took place, I had decided to wear my new green soft contact lenses. Not knowing when I picked up Harry to go to the hospital that we would be detained so long, it became the day I experienced the pain of shrinkage. There wasn't much I could have done about it anyway. My other lenses were at home, and even if I had had them with me, there was no way they could have been a viable substitute. By this time, the pain was too excruciating to assault my eyes with such irritating objects as gas permeable lenses. Besides, I thought, Harry is the one suffering. By 3:30 PM, the time I left his room and entered the elevator, the pain in my eyes was unbearable. No wonder a young woman looked at me and said, "Your eyes, what is wrong with them?"

I explained the problem to her and asked how she knew. She replied, "Your whites are completely red!"

I must have looked like an alien from another planet. Driving home in the bright August sunlight, I had to almost completely cover my eyes to shield them—and still navigate my way. When I got home, I drew the blinds and waited for my eyes to recover. In the darkness of the house, I thought about how brave Harry had been and wondered what was next for him.

That evening, I called Ken to tell him what Harry had been through. I also asked him to visit Harry. I was not shocked by his answer—I was offended. He said, "Sorry, kid, you're on your own."

I'll never know why he was not there for Harry, and for me. We had been through so much together, and after all, he was the one who had brought Harry and me together. How dare he do that to me! At that moment, I made a bitter resolution. And I struck out on my own from that day forward, to singularly prove that I didn't need Ken's help or anyone else's. It was my battle in the first place.

When I next visited Harry at the hospital, instead of telling me how he was progressing, he asked where I had parked my car. He made sure that I didn't stay after dark— which in August is fairly late— as the neighborhood wasn't safe. I was already feeling more attached to this young fighter than I knew I should be. When I saw his dinner still on his tray, long past mealtime, I asked if the food was inedible. He said it wasn't, except that it was too cold to eat, so I told him I would take it to the microwave seven floors below. He said, "They won't let you take food out of the room of an AIDS patient."

To which I replied, "We'll just see."

No one stopped me at any stage of my mission; not leaving the room, not walking down the hall to the elevator, not on the elevator, not on the first floor heading for the microwave facilities. And not at any of the same stations along the same route back to Harry's room. I wondered if that was good or bad. Good because the food was then warm enough to be eaten, bad because it seemed as if the hospital staff wasn't doing its job. After all of that, at least it was gratifying to see Harry eating his meal, if that can be said for hospital food.

At least six of Harry's close friends were checking on him regularly, some staying into the night until he fell asleep. Knowing he was in their good hands, I didn't go to see him for a few days. Then I received a message that he had checked himself out of the hospital, to make room for someone who "needed it more than he did." That concept of his didn't last long. He was admitted again two days later. His friends— Shawn, Joe (not the same Joe I knew before), and a few others—were taking turns being with him, so I didn't return until I received a message that Harry wanted to see me. It flattered me to know that he had chosen my company, rather than my deciding for myself when to visit him. I felt a sense of urgency from that phone call, and it was not unfounded. It was a rainy Friday night, and I had assumed that his friends had left me alone with him, possibly so they could go out to dinner or the bars for the evening. I didn't know what they did for entertainment. They were young gay men whose only activities I had witnessed were their kind acts of devotion to their friend, whom they knew would not be a part of their circle for very long. Actually, they were down the hall in the solarium, allowing me to have Harry to myself.

I asked him if he wanted his back rubbed. That was met with hearty approval. As I tried to be gentle, Harry kept pleading, "Harder, harder."

His voice was strong, and I felt comfortable at least with the fact that he was getting enough oxygen from the tube going into his nose. That didn't last long, though. Within an hour, Harry began to complain that what he called the oxygen machine wasn't working properly because he was having trouble breathing. Again, it seemed to me that he wasn't receiving much attention from the nursing staff. I don't recall them entering the room when I was there. At that point, though, together Harry and I decided it was time to change that. When the nurse saw that Harry was gasping for air, she called for the doctor, who gave Harry some options. By then, Shawn, Joe, and the other friends were gathered in the room. The doctor told Harry that he could attach him to a ventilator, where he would remain for the rest of his life, or he could administer morphine, from which he might not awaken the next morning.

Harry recovered his vocal skills enough to shout loudly, "What was my first option?"

"If we put you on a ventilator, you will never get off of it."

"And the other option, again?"

"You may not ever see your friends again. If we set up a morphine drip, you may die tonight."

"Will I live long enough to see my mother? She lives in Pennsylvania and is coming in on Tuesday. She has to see her doctor on Monday."

"I don't know, Harry. I cannot answer that question."

"And the first option?"

"You may live long enough to see your mother."

"I'll take the ventilator then."

It seemed that all hell broke loose. Harry was getting attention then. Orderlies rushed in to move the other beds in the room out of the way. Harry shared the room with three other AIDS patients; one of them a Hispanic man, who asked me, "¿Como se llama, el?"

What is his name? I understood that much of the language. "Harry," I replied.

He immediately grabbed his Spanish language Bible and began to pray aloud, inserting Harry's name wherever the reader was required to fill in the blank.

David, the young man in the bed next to Harry's, began compulsively to clean the room, even though he hobbled about from an AIDS-related infection in his left leg. He was frantic from what was happening around him. He also knew it would soon be his turn.

While we waited for Harry to be moved to the intensive care unit, his friends were out in the hall. I held Harry in my arms, and he spilled out the most important message he left behind.

"Tell my friends goodbye, tell my mother goodbye, and tell my dog goodbye."

I promised I would carry out his wishes. When he was gone from the room, I sat in the chair beside the now empty space where his bed had been, and wept.

David began to tell me his own background story; how he was born into a wealthy family who disowned him when they learned he was gay. There were many siblings and many rivalries, and he was spending the last days of his young life in a charity hospital. He feared dying alone. Why was this not new to me?

The next day, I learned that I was not on the short list of visitors who were allowed to see Harry in the ICU. That had to be all right; we had said our goodbyes. His friends—the same four or five who had kept vigil at the hospital, whether in his room or not—kept me informed of Harry's deteriorating condition. On Tuesday morning, upon exiting the elevator on the ICU floor, I encountered two women, one of whom had to be Harry's mother. She had brought her sister and daughter with her, but Harry's sister was not present at the moment. They looked out of place in a public hospital. Both women, who apparently were grateful for my attention to their loved one, greeted me warmly.

"You must be the girl who took Harry out for a picnic. He told me that he enjoyed it so much, and that you have been so nice to him," said his mother.

Besides improving my comfort level, having not known how his mother would feel about my intervention and maternal attention to her son, it didn't hurt that she had referred to me as a "girl." I had a son who was older than hers. We spent several hours together at the hospital, where I tried to comfort her. I thought about Gary, and had a slight feeling of survivor's guilt, yet at the same time I didn't want the inevitable reason for giving it up. The most powerful feeling I was experiencing in the dreary visitor's lounge was how much Harry meant to me. I loved him immensely.

The following week, a group of coworkers from my office were at Richard's house to help him with the construction of a convention booth. Richard was going to take our resident expert to Dallas to demonstrate a new, computerized, floor space-measuring device our design firm had recently installed. We were all out on the front lawn, with yards of fabric stretched out on the grass. Some of us were cutting it to size, to cover the display modules being built on the driveway. During all of this exciting activity, a wave of intuitive dread came over me, and I felt the need to call my office for phone messages. I was not surprised to discover that Ken had called to tell me that Harry was gone.

Why, I wondered, was he back in Harry's picture?

By then, it didn't matter that he had left me on my own to help Harry. He was there now and that was what counted. We hadn't time for petty fallouts. We were all pretty worn out. Dottie reappeared on the scene to take charge of Harry's funeral. At first, Harry's mother was grateful because she needed help. First, she had just lost her son, and second, she was not familiar with the city enough to know which funeral home to call or where to hold the service. I was notified a few days later that it was to be held in the same Baptist church where Dottie had previously taken Harry, regardless of the fact that he was a Methodist. Though I resented the choice of venues, I was comforted by the fact that the Baptist church had opened an AIDS ministry. It had previously turned away from the problem.

Joe, Shawn, and Harry's other friends, whom I had met at the hospital, sat a few rows behind Harry's mother, aunt, and sister. I, sitting behind them, sensed from their body language that there was something bothering them besides Harry's death itself. My personal reactions were that, not only did it dumbfound me that Dottie had chosen this particular church, but also that the pastor continually praised Dottie for her generosity of spirit in her work with Harry and other PWAs. This was Harry's memorial service, not Dottie's pep rally! It reminded me of Novelette's funeral.

I spotted David, the lame young man who had frantically cleaned the hospital room after Harry had been taken to the intensive care unit. When the minister called for people to come forward and share their stories about their relationship with Harry, David, looking old beyond his years, struggled forward leaning on his cane. At the foot of the stairs to the podium, he prostrated himself, sobbing. Remembering our encounter in the hospital such a short time ago, and noticing how his appearance had so rapidly changed, I wept for David and mourned for Harry.

After the funeral service, at which Harry's body was not present, I spoke with Harry's mother and aunt. I invited them to have lunch the next afternoon and they agreed. Although by then I had accumulated more experience than I ever wanted in the realm of pseudo pastoral care, I was not professionally trained for it. The realization that I was merely a volunteer made me apprehensive during lunch. After all, I didn't know these women. Sure, we had a substantial bond, but because of my discomfort at the service the previous night, I prepared myself for the worst. I was afraid they might criticize something for which I wouldn't have an adequate response. Apparently, all three of us were on the same wavelength. Harry's mother turned to me and asked, "What did you think of the service?"

"I thought it was more about Dottie than Harry."

"That's what I noticed, too," she replied.

Harry's aunt agreed. None of us understood why the minister repeatedly praised Dottie for all she had done for Harry. Not that she hadn't been there for him sometimes, but it was his service and we were there to honor Harry, not Dottie. The inappropriate attention did not go unnoticed.

The next night, a large group of Harry's friends met for dinner at the same restaurant which Ken and I had frequented so often. Harry's aunt announced that her husband had instructed her to treat all of us to dinner, in appreciation for what we had done for Harry. It was a lovely gesture.

Someone in the group announced that Dottie had said she would arrive late. Apparently confusing that news with the knowledge that Harry's mother intended to take Harry's ashes back to Pennsylvania with her for burial, I thought that perhaps Dottie was going to make a grand entrance and hand over to Harry's mother an envelope filled with Harry's ashes. I had never before seen how human ashes were presented to the family. I pictured an envelope, which was not delivered; nor were Harry's ashes presented in a container of any kind when Dottie arrived.

Shame on me!

The next afternoon, we were off and running. His mother and aunt sifted through Harry's few possessions and decided what they wanted to keep. They quickly realized there was too much to take on the plane with them, and decided to give away things they didn't particularly care about. I didn't feel good about taking anything. I realized I had been accumulating the remnants of too many unfulfilled dreams, too many memories of lost friends. It began to feel like a trophy collection—and what dubious trophies they were. I couldn't do it anymore.

I was physically and emotionally exhausted as we went through Harry's belongings, which I offered to ship to Pennsylvania. After driving downtown to my office for boxes and packing tape, and returning to Harry's apartment, they packed two large cardboard boxes and called it a day. And I called Federal Express.

We had promised to stay in touch with each other. Four months later I sent them a Christmas card, but never heard back from them. I was sure my earthly connection with Harry was over. But during one of my many visits to the Names Project quilt display, feeling grateful that I hadn't recognized any of the names on the panels, one suddenly caught my eye. There were only two words on it—Harry's first and last names. It was the only one of its kind in simplicity; no dates, no memorable events, no photograph; just his name. I don't know who made it, but seeing it tore into me and caused me to vow never to go to another one of those exhibits, and I haven't.

1986

28.
Michael 4 and Michael 5—A Couple

Perhaps it was time. By the time Harry died, I felt that my mission had been completed. I had held the last hand, rubbed the last back, shed my last tears, and smiled my last determined smile. I was so passionate about my relationship with Harry that I couldn't conceive of going through that grueling exercise again. Besides, I wasn't getting any more assignments from the AIDS Foundation. In retrospect, I don't even recall a conscious effort on my part to distance myself from them. It must have occurred when I wasn't looking, because I was certainly caught up in the AIDS community, with more people who needed help and social events that wouldn't quit. One thing I learned about gay people: they liked having a good time, eating good food, and celebrating life, whether it was their own or that of someone who had passed on to their eternal gala.

By the end of 1986, after three intense years of meeting, loving, and losing one young brave soul after another, I knew I had to step back—long enough, at least, to take a deep breath. Surely, that would enable me to decide where to go from there.

After Ken told me I was on my own during Harry's illness, I had resolved to become more independent in my commitment to serve the AIDS community. I developed a stronger sense of autonomy, and my relationship to Ken changed to one of ambivalence. We continued to see each other, but I no longer felt the need to be one half of a unit. There was no bitterness or resentment, just occasional singularity. It didn't keep us from interacting in our work, or our socialization.

When Ken and I attended a late afternoon New Year's Eve party on a dark and cold Wednesday, I was unknowingly not only entering a new calendar year, but also bridging the gap of uncertainty in my work and involvement with AIDS. Until we arrived, I hadn't realized that the party was at the home of one of the AIDS nurses, the same person who had been the facilitator of Jan's support group. I had crossed paths with this nurse many times over the past few years, and when I realized whose party I was attending, I was immediately put at ease. By the time Ken and I had eaten more hors d'oeuvres than we should have, visited with people, and taken our leave, we decided there wasn't much point in going out to dinner. We headed to the popular bar where Truman and I had spent so many evenings after Bob died.

There was nothing particularly memorable about the time we spent at the bar, except for meeting a couple of Ken's friends whose names were Michael and Michael. One was very tall, with blue eyes that sparkled when he smiled. He was wearing a cowboy hat and boots, and blue jeans. He was incredibly handsome and seemed self-assured. The other Michael was shorter, with slicked-down black hair and an impeccably groomed mustache. He was wearing a gorgeous black suit that I took to be a tuxedo. He looked like he had just stepped out of a photo shoot. We visited for a while with them and left. The significant aspect of the event for me was that it became the segue to another extremely intense relationship.

As time passed, I became less of a social appendage of Ken's and more assured of my own ability to form bonds with people, even the ones I met through him. So it was not unlikely that the Michaels and I would become close friends. They invited me to their home many times for dinner and it became a Friday night ritual, unless we went out to dinner at their favorite Mexican restaurant. At first, their two schnauzers yapped incessantly when I first entered the house. But before long, they would not only greet me excitedly by jumping all over me, they eventually found comfort in my lap.

Michael B. was retired from a large chemical company due to his HIV status, although he had a few years left before he even turned forty. He was an excellent cook, and it was great to come "home" from work every Friday night to dinner that was ready and waiting for the other Michael and me.

It was refreshing to see a young man who took such pride in his appearance as Michael D. What I had perceived as his special New Year's Eve attire was actually how he dressed for work every day. What a clotheshorse he was.

One Friday night, we rented the movie *Longtime Companion*. I was lying on the floor (so my anticipated crying wouldn't be so conspicuous), while the Michaels watched from their chairs. In the scene where one character says to his dying companion, "It's okay to let go," I latched on to that line—knowing that someday I would probably be saying those words myself. When I heard Michael D. bawling uncontrollably, I let go and cried openly. My bond with these two was gaining strength, and that strength would soon be tested.

Another year passed and another Christmas arrived. By then, I was very comfortable with my new friends. They invited me to help them decorate their tree, and to take down the decorations a week later. New Year's Eve rolled around again; I had already known them for a year. Since it was a special occasion, we decided we could forego Mexican food for a change, so we went to a lovely steakhouse—just Michael, Michael, and I. After dinner, as we headed to the parking lot, we talked about Michael D.'s upcoming birthday and what we would do to celebrate it. These men were still in their thirties. I was considerably ahead of them age-wise. Thinking it clever, I said, "I don't want to get to forty."

It was too late. I had said it. Michael B. looked at me, his twinkling eyes now somber, and said, "I do."

Damn! Why did I say that? Fortunately for me, our friendship endured. We continued to spend a lot of time together at various events around the mostly gay neighborhood. At one street fair, I borrowed money from Michael B. because I just had to have a spiral plastic rainbow on a wire to hang on my porch. I didn't know for more than ten years that it was a meaningful symbol to the gay community.

Easter dinner was wonderful. Michael B. had prepared it for us and we were joined by his father, who was very loving and supportive of his son. He and I had a lot in common because of HIV, and I was equally comfortable when we were invited to his house for dinner.

However, Michael B. was apparently wearing down. One night when the other Michael returned home from work, he found a note on the newel of the staircase: "Don't go upstairs." Of course, he went upstairs. He found his lover in the bathtub, unconscious from an overdose of medication. The police were called and Michael was taken to the hospital. He had actually gone to the neighborhood pawnshop that morning and purchased a pistol, which was found on the side of the tub, but had passed out from the overdose before using the gun. He had strategically placed his will and other important papers on the kitchen table before going upstairs to end his life.

By the time I was allowed to visit him, he was extremely

depressed. The sparkle never came back. He explained the reason for his attempted suicide was that he was just so very, very tired. He didn't want to fight it anymore.

As time moved along, tension grew between the Michaels and, as I heard, Michael D. was asked by the other's parents to leave the beautiful home they had created together. I didn't know what had happened to cause the breakup. When I last visited Michael B., while he was in the hospital for an AIDS-related illness, I was at a loss for words and we both floundered in our conversation. It was the first time I had felt so uncomfortable by the bedside of someone in his condition. And we had been such close friends. What was happening?

It was very disturbing to me that I simply lost touch with him, and didn't know he had died until Michael D. called to inform me. I was extremely angry with myself for exiting that relationship the way I did. I wanted his parents to know that I cared, but hesitated to call. My written condolences went unacknowledged.

1987-1992

29.
Time with Gary

S ince Gary worked within the university system, at least one week of his vacation always fell during the week between Christmas and New Year's Day, when the on-campus laboratory where he worked was closed for the holidays. The vacation choice for the winter of 1986 was skiing near Reno, Nevada, and I experienced the thrill of downhill skiing. I knew that I could break a leg—or, God forbid, even my neck—but charged ahead, willing to do anything to please my son. I suspected that his life would end before mine, and I wanted to be there for whatever he was willing to share with me.

Of course, in the evenings we frequented the casinos, and while I fed the starving slot machines, Gary patiently sat on a stool playing computerized blackjack. He didn't require the clanging bells, whistles, and miniskirted waitresses trying to sell him drinks. He was happy to apply his mathematical mind to accumulating his silent winnings until we retreated to our hotel room for the night. We had chosen Reno because one of the hotels there had placed a very intriguing ad in the *San Francisco Chronicle* offering $25.00 worth of chips per day to guests of the hotel. With Gary winning practically every game he played, we left Reno having paid a hotel bill of only $10.00. He was not only very happy but also very healthy.

The next year, we tried that again at a different ski resort in Nevada, but the temperature was so bitterly cold that Gary—after a few trial runs down the slopes while I waited in the lodge, drinking hot chocolate—decided he had had enough of that kind of fun. His stamina was holding up, but he didn't want to overextend himself. There was no evidence of any health problems, and he prided himself on being in a study group of long-term survivors who were sure to beat the virus at its own game.

1986

***

In 1988, a Halloween party in New Orleans—where Gary had held his first job, at Shell Oil, after graduating from college—brought him near enough to Texas to warrant a visit with me. We organized a family picnic, at which he was prepared to announce his AIDS status and face whatever scrutiny might have confronted him.

My brother and his family, who had initially shown no interest in Gary's illness or my struggling with it, attended, as well as the rest of my family who lived in the city. There was no tension or need for Gary to deliver his rehearsed speech.

It was the last time Gary was in Texas, and for most of the family, the last time they would ever see him.

30.
Back to Steve

During the period when the AIDS Foundation was reorganizing and reassigning volunteers as individual buddies instead of teams, Steve, one of the original team members, became a very active "buddy," and we stayed connected by telephone, dinners, and movies. I was still working very closely with Ken, yet I always had time for Steve. But after he moved to Dallas, the only connection we had was our Friday afternoon phone chats. It was during one of these conversations that we set up a dinner date to be followed by a play during his next visit to Houston. When the day arrived, I was dressed, ready, and waiting. And waiting, and waiting. I heard nothing from Steve. And that was the end of the reliability he had demonstrated when I was first getting to know him.

He called many months later to apologize, and explained that he had had a drinking problem but was past that. I was quite shocked to hear about it, but it explained his irrational behavior of making dates and breaking them. I had never observed any evidence of it during the many times we had been together.

Not long after I last spoke with Steve, I was ironing clothes one evening while watching the television show *Midnight Caller*, starring Gary Cole. I liked seeing him because he reminded me of Steve. When the phone rang that Tuesday night, I really didn't want to answer it, but something compelled me to do so. Much to my surprise, it was Paul, Steve's lover who had moved to Paris. He was back in town after having visited Steve in Dallas for the weekend. The news was not good. He told me that they had spent an enjoyable weekend together, but on Monday, when Steve didn't show up for work or call the office, his coworkers called his home and there was no answer. Considering that strange enough to prompt them to go to his apartment the next morning, they found him dead. Paul promised me that he would let me know what happened, but I never heard from him again. I wrote to Steve's mother in California, but didn't hear from her, either. I couldn't believe that another one of my dear friends was gone. He was only thirty-eight years old.

To the best of my knowledge, Steve was HIV-negative.

1989

31.
Another Fred—Another Tim

The formation of the AIDS Foundation during the early years involved a series of incarnations as the needs of the AIDS community developed. So it was inevitable that the original group of volunteers, in addition to the new ones coming on board, would be subject to participating in more than one weekend training session. We exchanged information about ourselves and our own experiences with AIDS. We did role-playing and traded personal secrets that were promised to be kept confidential. The importance of confidentiality in everything we said or did in relation to AIDS was repeatedly stressed to us, because of the need for privacy and anonymity. It was not uncommon for people to become disenfranchised if it was discovered that they were infected with the virus.

During the second training weekend I attended, there was an incredibly handsome young man named Fred—a new Fred in my life—who was described by the men in our group as "knuckle-biting good-looking." Though he must have been fully aware of his physical attributes, he was very modest and friendly. When it was Fred's turn to play the role of a caregiver to a critically ill person with AIDS whom he was visiting in the hospital, I thought I would die of heartbreak. I watched the young man lying still on the floor while Fred leaned over him, and spoke quietly and gently of how he cared about what was happening to the "person with AIDS." As hard as I tried to remain stoic, it was too much for me, and I broke down and bawled. I wasn't the only one in the room reacting to the scene we had witnessed. By that time, I had already had such actual experiences, because the original team I belonged to had been in the field for two years. Watching Fred and his co-actor caused a flood of memories to wash through my soul.

I was fortunate to gain Fred as a friend, and spent much of my free time with him. On one occasion, Fred attended a baseball game as my guest at a company outing. When he picked me up that day, I noticed how thin he looked and that he was experiencing symptoms of a cold or the flu. He loved playing baseball and attending professional games, so we had a good time that day, but I could tell that he was not well. It wasn't long before Fred's health deteriorated and took him from the category of *us*, the worried well, to *them*, those with AIDS. My memories of Fred's acting skills at the training weekend became all too real and rushed back in when I learned that Fred had died.

One of Gary's closest friends, Tim, whom I had encountered at Billy's bedside a few years before, was at Fred's funeral. As the mourners exited the front of the church after offering condolences to Fred's heartbroken family, Tim and I spotted each other and grieved for our mutual loss. Fred had been Tim's therapist, I learned that day.

Usually, when you encounter someone with whom you agree to stay in touch, it just doesn't happen. But when I suggested to Tim that we spend some time together, he responded with, "How about tonight?"

It was the beginning of a very special friendship.

Tim arrived that very night. My only memory of our first social visit, with no mutual friends or relatives, was that I sat on the couch and Tim sprawled, facedown, on the carpeted floor as we listened to *Hearts of Space* together, neither of us speaking for the duration of the hour. Not long after that first lovely evening we spent together, I received a letter from Gary, which included the following paragraph:

"Tim wrote and said he enjoyed his visit with you. He remarked that he never noticed so many similarities between you and me. I suppose it's not so surprising since we've been so close for so long. Let's keep it that way!"

Gary and Tim had met in college and become very close friends, together with another man named Neal. They were like The Three Musketeers. After Gary moved to New Orleans to take his first job after college graduation, Neal and I formed a friendship of our own. I still see Neal when he performs with the Gay Men's Chorus, but we no longer socialize. Having Fred as our common denominator in 1988, Tim and I began an intensely close relationship, as he informed me that he, too, was HIV-positive.

It wasn't long before we were calling each other frequently and meeting for dinner. We didn't talk about Gary; we had our own friendship based on our mutual interests, problems, and dynamics. On one occasion, we were in a cafeteria having dinner. I poured out some of my most personal anguish, before considering whether or not it was appropriate to share with Tim. His response bonded us even closer. He said, "I am very flattered that you are willing to share such intimate feelings with me." It provided a permanent bond that would endure between us.

At that time, Tim was living in a beautiful two-story townhouse with a friend named Mike, who was living with AIDS. Their agreement had been that Tim would live in Mike's home, rent-free, and take care of Mike and the house until Mike died. With neither of them knowing when that would occur, Tim was enjoying Mike's generosity—albeit with mixed feelings of gratitude and apprehension. In what I thought was a rather casual conversation, Tim asked if he could move in with me after Mike died. Without hesitation, I told him, "Sure, it'll be fun."

During that year, 1988, we saw a lot of movies, ate a lot of cafeteria food, and shared a lot about ourselves. Tim brought a kind of Walden Pond appreciation into my life. He encouraged me to go to an arboretum in the city and sit by the lake, which had ducks of all sizes and other creatures typically found in a natural habitat in southeast Texas. I hadn't known until then that there was such a lake so close to home. One night, we drove to an ideal spot to watch a lunar eclipse. Nature was a large part of Tim's life, and he taught me to appreciate it more than I ever had. We visited another arboretum, where I found eighteen pennies neatly stacked on the ground in the parking lot when I opened my car door—a trivial but memorable event. This large oasis on the outskirts of Houston was nestled near the major airport north of town. The natural beauty, with the air scented by the many herbs in their own special garden, and the cacophony of jet engines was a dichotomy that jarred our senses. Ah, nature!

Then came the big freeze of February 1989, an extremely rare phenomena in this part of the country.

Almost all of my coworkers left the office early, to get safely home before the traffic made it impossible, and I chose to ride with the one remaining person. Our plan was to go to his house, where we would wait until the heavy traffic cleared; then he would drive me home. We had no trouble with the traffic, so we decided to stop for dinner. That went well, but upon arriving at his apartment complex, I stepped out of the car and slipped on the ice, sustaining a serious break to my wrist. Wallowing in pain for three days—alone—came to a halt the following Saturday morning. As I padded around the house in my nightgown, oversized robe, and slippers, the sound of the doorbell was not very welcome.

There stood Tim, looking great in his best suit. Before I even opened the screen door for him to come in from the cold, he asked, "Is the invitation still open? I just came from Mike's funeral."

What could I say? At the moment, I didn't really feel like committing to having a roommate. I had never had one before, and the prospect of having one right then wasn't very appealing. We talked about it and agreed that there was plenty of time to implement the details of his move. Having promised that he would wind up Mike's affairs, sell the condo, and tie up loose ends, he could stay there as long as he wanted. I had not been to the condo yet, but that would soon change.

Three weeks later, I was laid off from my job of twenty-one years, due to the company's loss of their major account during the collapse of the savings and loan industry and its trickle-down effect on retail stores. They no longer needed the services of our design firm. Once my broken arm healed, I would have an abundance of time to devote to my AIDS volunteer work.

By that time, I had climbed out of the trenches to work with the Mail Team. There was always a huge amount of work for that group as the AIDS Foundation grew. We were either soliciting funds, announcing a fund-raising event, or both, within the same mail-out. We usually met in the evening after the team members who had paying jobs finished their daily work. It was fun for a lot of reasons; the team leader usually brought Pee-wee Herman tapes and popcorn, and in spite of the dire purpose of our gathering, we had a good time while we worked. And we didn't have to concentrate heavily on the task at hand, as long as we kept the ZIP codes properly separated. There were usually thousands of pieces to be collated, folded, and stuffed into envelopes. We attached the mailing labels before sending them all through the postage machine and cramming them into bags provided by the postal service. Sometimes a single mailing job took two or three days to complete.

After proving how efficient I was at that job, I was given independent tasks to do during the daytime, since my lack of employment gave me so much "leisure" time. I was left alone, with little or no supervision, to complete whatever task had been assigned by the person in charge of volunteer activities. Sometimes that involved viewing the highly classified volunteer files to remove superfluous paper, which was accumulating faster than anyone could keep up with it. I was privy to information about my fellow volunteers which had to be kept strictly confidential. There was a lot of potential gossip, but it was fortunate that my training and practice regarding confidentiality was in full force. Although interesting, the material was a nonissue.

One frustrating chore was assembling leaflets of HIV/ AIDS information together with packages of condoms into unmarked manila folders, to be passed out to gay bar patrons on Friday and Saturday nights. The frustration was that when I opened the huge cardboard carton of condoms, I saw hundreds of what looked like chocolate coins wrapped in shiny gold foil. They were condoms; I wanted chocolate!

At the annual volunteer appreciation party, I was chosen as the Volunteer of the Year, and was chastised for not attending the party to accept my award. I said that, had I known I was to receive it, I would have attended, and was told, "We wanted it to be a surprise."

I wish I had gone.

In spite of my unofficial resignation from direct care and advocacy, there was always someone who inadvertently came into my life who needed care and attention.

While I was heavily involved at the AIDS Foundation office, Tim worked as a florist—a job demanding long hours, even after closing time, because of the necessity of cleaning up the shop before the next day's business messed it up again. He was also trying to fulfill the commitment he had made to Mike. Due to his overburdened schedule, he occasionally asked me to stand in for him at Mike's condo, to meet with some of the by-appointment-only estate sale customers. I remember the serenity I found there, drowsing to the sound of light rain, mountain brooks, even white noise, all emanating from the "noise machine" from The Sharper Image. The grand piano in the corner, always covered with a lovely drape and graced with a huge vase of fresh flowers, had to be sold. The crystal stemware, the huge collection of Beta tapes (no longer playable), the incredibly comfortable furniture—all had to go. But in the meantime, Tim and I met there on many occasions to sit by the pool and get closer to each other.

Another of my sisters-in-law, who had been diagnosed the previous August with pancreatic cancer, was failing in her battle, so my time and attention shifted to a different front. As devastating and heartbreaking as AIDS had become in my life, I was reminded that it was not the only disease which took its toll on people and their families. In fact, I had only two years prior, and four years before that, lost two other family members to cancer. My training with the AIDS community came in very handy. But it didn't last long; by June, my beloved sister-in-law was gone, only ten months after her diagnosis. Shortly after her death, my brother began a long, muddled period of calling me frequently, interspersed with unannounced visits. Unbeknownst to anyone, he was on a collision course with Alzheimer's disease. I was feeling the burden of responsibility for him that should have been—but I thought wasn't—shared by the rest of my family. I was simultaneously scared and resentful, and I didn't like myself very much for those feelings. But I, too, was going down my own road—to severe depression.

It was in the midst of this total chaos for me that Tim said he was ready to move in. I had made the commitment to him and had to abide by it, but I surely wasn't ready. By the time he had settled in to what had been Gary's bedroom, I was silently screaming inside. My brother called nearly every morning, and since Tim's room was closer to the phone, he answered it and hollered to me down the long hallway, "It's your brother!"

My nerves were shattered. My poor brother didn't realize that his visits and calls were not welcome at the time. Neither the rest of my family nor I realized what was wrong with him. I just wasn't ready to take that on at the same time as having a new roommate. It felt strange, as I had never lived with anyone who was not family.

It took some getting used to, having someone living under my roof. Even though we had an agreed-upon set of house rules, I was no longer comfortable in my own home. I had never before closed my bedroom door at night, and now felt confined by doing so. I huddled on the floor in there to watch TV, sitting close to the set so I could keep the volume down. I was staying in the bedroom later and later every morning to avoid facing the day—until, of course, the inevitable phone call that came every midmorning.

Tim set up his paints and airbrush equipment in the backyard in order to produce his original, and quite lovely, greeting cards and stationery, which he planned to sell. He was artistically talented in many areas besides floral design. Having a similar background, I should have enjoyed every minute of it, but I was fading fast. He went about his residence in my house with good cheer and apparent contentment, and expressed those feelings by surprising me with exquisite floral arrangements which he left in my bedroom when I was out. Coming home to those sweet sentiments melted my heart, but what was wrong with me? I was falling apart.

One morning, I escaped to the screened-in porch, but within minutes, Tim approached and asked if I wanted to talk.

"No," I said abruptly.

"Well, I'm willing to discuss anything with anyone, if they want to."

That was exactly what I needed, and it all came pouring out. I was completely exhausted. I explained that it was difficult to have someone living with me, particularly while I was so worried about both Gary's health and my brother's frequent surprise visits. Tim very graciously offered to spend more time with his new boyfriend, Dan.

1988-1989

32.

Intermission

By September 1989, while Tim was still living with me, my anxiety was building. I found myself in the office of a mental health therapist, who insisted that I see the psychiatrist with whom she worked. The next day, I returned to the same office to see the doctor, reeling from anxiety and well-founded fear. He advised me to check into a psychiatric hospital immediately. I insisted that I had to go to visit Gary in San Francisco at the end of the month, because I had promised my sister I would go with her when she arrived from Israel. She had enjoyed the visit both Garys and I made five years earlier, and was eager to see them again. That was the end of that doctor and his recommendation. But I was on the edge of collapse.

After my sister visited with family in Texas, she and I headed west. The view from the plane revealed the beauty of jigsaw puzzle pieces of colors and shapes formed by the intermingling of adjacent crops far below. It was scenery to calm the soul. Aspen trees, their leaves quaking and shimmering in the autumn sunlight in such abundance resembled a gigantic spread of golden jewelry over Colorado, thousands of feet below.

It was September 26, a very important day for Gary. We had barely arrived at his house, and the telephone rang while he was carrying our luggage up the fourteen outside stairs, so

I answered. It was my niece, who lived in Santa Cruz. She had just received word that Gary C. had died that day and was calling to console my Gary, although he had not yet heard about it. Only once had I seen Gary C. after he was diagnosed with AIDS. I don't know when that occurred, and I was so wrapped up in my own son's condition that, I regret to admit, I didn't think too much more about it. But now, there we were, standing in the kitchen while Gary listened to his cousin as she gave him the news. After slowly replacing the receiver in its cradle, he stoically went about carrying mattresses from the basement, again up the fourteen stairs, through the front door, down the hall, and into the parlor, where he placed them together for my sister and me.

The three of us went to the store to buy groceries for the coming week, and throughout the entire evening Gary didn't say anything about the death of his former lover. Even though they had ended their intimate relationship a few years before, they were still very close friends. Two nights later, at a gathering for friends and family of Gary C.'s, my sister contributed memories of him with her recollections of their connection when the two Garys and I had visited Israel. I hadn't known that they had been corresponding during the five years since our visit, so she was quite prepared to speak of their relationship. I felt that his family appreciated her participation, as did I, since I was hesitant that she might feel out of place with them. I have only recently come to realize that I didn't give my son the attention and comfort he deserved at that time, and I deeply regret my omission. I should have encouraged him to talk about his loss if he wanted to, or at least expressed my sympathy to him. I was so engrossed in my own miserable depression that I completely overlooked my son's feelings.

Gary was a gracious host, taking us to see the sights in

and around his city. We spent a few days in Santa Cruz and drove down the coast road to Big Sur.

By October 3, after taking my sister to the airport to continue her visit with other relatives in the U.S., both Gary and I were emotionally tired. It was then that he informed me that he had reluctantly just begun taking AZT. We both knew that it might produce harmful side effects, and he had avoided it for as long as he felt he could juggle the consequences of either decision. If he didn't take the medication, his health might have deteriorated further; yet, if he took AZT, he might have suffered from its toxicity. He felt nauseated and uneasy from the drug, but he persevered. As we sat atop Corona Heights looking down over San Francisco, I thought my heart would break for him, but I knew that I had to leave in a few days to return home.

October 17 was my brother's birthday. After spending the day with him, taking him to two different doctors, and then trying to help him light the furnace—which by this time, in his declining mental health state, was difficult for him—I left him in the company of another of my brothers, to go to the AIDS Foundation for an evening of volunteer work. I enjoyed the camaraderie of the other volunteers—some of whom were serving out their court-ordered community service for minor infractions of the law—and the comfort of the work itself. As the group dispersed for the evening, someone announced that they had just heard news that the Golden Gate Bridge had fallen into San Francisco Bay. There had been a major earthquake, which caused the Bay Bridge, not the Golden Gate, to collapse. That was very bad news to me, because I knew Gary crossed that bridge every day to get to work in Berkeley, and to get back home to the city. I couldn't get home fast enough to find out if he was all right.

My answering machine tape revealed first a message from my sister who lives in Houston. She gave the date, clarified that it was our brother's birthday, and asked if we had any plans for a celebration. Next was a message from a friend informing me of the earthquake. Where was Gary's voice? Finally, the third message was from Gary, and detailed the events he had experienced. He had just gotten home when he felt a rolling sensation in the concrete floor of his garage. When he realized what was happening, he ran out into the street, lest the house collapse on him. Then he realized that the power lines might fall, so he found a safer spot. He was anxious to go inside and see if there was any damage caused by the quake, because he had recently finished installing earthquake bracing and wanted to know if it had worked. Apparently, it had; only one small vase fell to the floor and broke. His relief was short-lived, as he began to think about his neighbors and their safety. For many years, he had stocked food and water for just such an occasion, and was willing and able to share it. Fortunately, it wasn't needed.

Gary had had the foresight to also call another brother of mine in Houston, who had one daughter living in Santa Cruz and another in San Jose—two cities cut off from each other and with no phone lines available to inform their family of their status. Apparently, they were not cut off from San Francisco. Gary wanted the family to know that its California members were safe.

The fourth and final message on my machine was from another friend, telling me of the earthquake and of his concern for my son. I immediately replaced that tape with a new one and saved it for posterity, because it was a dated historical event in our lives, and particularly because I can hear Gary's voice over and over again. But I haven't had the courage to listen to it.

1989

33.
Third Gary Loss

Although Gary, the therapist, had shared with me that he did not want to be tested for the AIDS virus, he appeared to be in good health for as long as I knew him. But for some reason, I had stopped seeing him in the summer of 1989. By December of that year, I knew that I needed mental health intervention. At the time, it had been well over a year since I had been laid off from my job. Fortunately, I had been rehired on a part-time basis, with enough working hours to qualify for the company group insurance plan. My job was to handle whatever duties were required to officially shut down the company (which would eventually take another fifteen years). But I needed help with my own faltering life. Having severed the brief relationship with the psychiatrist who had suggested hospitalization in September, I frantically searched through the preferred providers manual of my health insurance plan.

My decision was to find a female therapist, as I felt another woman might relate better to my desperation. Choosing the first one I found in the book, I dialed her number and hoped for the best. After a few minutes of briefing her on my lifelong problems—now festering into what I felt was an explosive crisis—she suggested I begin seeing her to, as she put it, "make you happy again."

My instinctive reaction was happy? Again? Neither word

had been in my psychological vocabulary. If "happy" had never existed, how could "again?"

Her name was Carol. What impressed me the most about our conversation was that she stayed on the phone with me for over twenty minutes—very unusual for someone in her field—and I was competent enough to know that was a good thing.

We began our sessions the following week, and I brought her up-to-date on Gary's diagnosis and what I had been doing the previous six years to prepare myself for it. Originally, my motivation was to meet the enemy head-on by becoming involved with AIDS volunteer work, but before long, I was consumed with it. My son was either coping quite well or just not telling me how it was affecting his daily life.

From the time that Gary made a unilateral decision years before to attend college in another city, I felt that my maternal role had changed from that of a nurturing parent, who had raised her child to become an independent adult, to one who knew when it was time to wish him well on his life journey. Due to our limited resources, I had assumed that he would live at home and go to a local college. When he announced to me, "I think I'll go to The University of Texas in Austin," I asked, "What made you arrive at that decision?"

He replied, "There comes a time in life when it's time to move on."

It was a small but powerful exchange, and brought to mind a little metaphoric lesson I had once read. "If a bird lands on the palm of your hand and you try to close your hand around it, it will surely fly away." I knew it was time for Gary to fly.

Because Gary had exercised his right as an adult, I sensed that if he wanted to tell me something, he would. I was really more afraid to ask questions of him, for fear of his refusal to answer. I had to weigh which discomfort I was willing to live with: that of not learning as much about him as I would have preferred to know, or the feeling of rejection.

It was the winter of 1989, and Gary had been very healthy for the past six years, so I chose to honor his desire to take care of himself, knowing that if he needed help, he would let me know. It was both an immense burden and a relief, because I knew I was really feeding my sense of denial. After all, if I didn't see his illness or hear about it, it didn't exist.

The following February, two days before my birthday, I received a call from Ken informing me that therapist Gary was in the hospital. How could that be? How did Ken know? How could I confirm it? After my frantic reaction had calmed, we agreed that I would call our friend Michael, a pharmacist, who knew everything about everybody. How could he not, having dispensed the bulk of the drugs to the gay community in the city at that time? There were many Michaels in my life by this time, and this Michael let me know that therapist Gary had not looked well the last time he had seen him in the drugstore. Now what should I do? My head was spinning; once again it seemed impossible to think clearly. Suddenly, I felt incredibly smart as I blurted out, "I know. I'll call the hospital."

However, I wasn't ready for the response from the nurse who took my call. I asked, "Do you have a patient named Gary T.?"

Matter-of-factly, she replied, "We did, but he expired this morning."

Jeez, I couldn't even cry. I was beyond devastated. He had told me only a few months earlier, "I'll be here if you need me." Now he wasn't!

I now had something else to talk about with Carol. It was my birthday, and I was trying to think of how to spend the rest of the day. As it happened, it was a good choice to go to the Museum of Fine Arts. I found dark exhibits where I could hide, meditate, and feel. I learned within a few days that it was where Gary T.'s lover worked, so I had inadvertently connected with him while paying my solitary respects.

1989-1990

34.

Club Med

Every spring, there is a grand celebration at a plush hotel in Houston to acknowledge those citizens chosen to receive the Mayor's Award for outstanding volunteer service to the community. After a lavish sit-down dinner, each honoree is called to the stage to receive their award from a wide variety of categories. I was invited to be the guest of Jack, the man who received the 1990 award for his work in the AIDS community. He was the volunteer who had celebrated the success of the big fund-raiser with me in 1984. It was a great honor for me simply to be included.

After the party ended and the guests were dispersing, my host turned to me and said, "You'd better keep your dance card open for tomorrow's event, too."

I hadn't been aware that, at another hotel chosen for the next evening's fundraising gala for the AIDS Foundation, Morgan Fairchild was to be the guest speaker. On that occasion, while my escort was mingling with people he knew, I visited the hosting committee's table to ask where I was to sit.

"You are sitting at Ms. Fairchild's table," a woman informed me.

Wow. How did I rate that? It soon became obvious that it was because I was with the person who had received the AIDS volunteer award the night before, and he was honored again by being assigned to her table.

During the cocktail hour, since my date had left me on my own, I strolled into the spacious lobby of the hotel and encountered Joe, my birthday-picture-taking host who had sent his lover, Tim, to his eternal reward in a table radio. I believe he was the self-appointed photographer for the evening, and it was good to see him again. Over five years had passed since our confrontation at the gathering after Danny had died, where Joe had chastised me for my refusal to notarize a blank document. There was no need to kiss and make up; time had healed that wound. Besides, I had forgotten about it, and perhaps so had Joe. It didn't matter; we were all too busy doing more important things in our crusade to end the fight against AIDS. We didn't need to have a secondary battlefield of our own.

Joe and I were just beginning to catch up, chatting about what we had been doing since we had last seen each other, when he abruptly interrupted me to announce, "And here's milady now."

With that, he stood and walked up to the guest of honor and her entourage.

When we were all seated for dinner, I was introduced to Morgan Fairchild and her family members who had accompanied her. She was very beautiful and gracious, and humored us with inside information about Hollywood, saying that she had learned many of her makeup tricks from gay men. She was obviously very comfortable in the AIDS community. Beginning her address to the large audience, she told us that she had originally been interested in entering the medical field, and subscribed to journals that kept her up-to-date on those matters of interest. Her awareness of HIV and AIDS had initially come from those sources.

After all the speeches, the musical entertainment, and an excellent dinner, Joe made the rounds and snapped photos of any and all who wanted a memorable keepsake of the evening, in addition to the perfume samples that were a part of each attendee's place setting. He took two pictures of me with Ms. Fairchild, which I showed to Richard at work the next day. He said, "You look great, kid. Who's the honey with you?"

Well! That was a quite a compliment. But when I identified the "honey," he still didn't know who she was.

She autographed dinner programs and I requested one for Gary. Her special message for him was, "Gary, I'm sorry I missed you tonight. Love, Morgan Fairchild." Since I was leaving in a few days to meet Gary for a five-day vacation at Club Med in Mexico, I was looking forward to presenting the personal message to him. Unfortunately, his response was much like Richard's. Even though Morgan Fairchild is an icon in the gay world, he didn't know who she was, either—most likely because he didn't watch television.

The next evening, I received a phone call from Kansas City informing me that one of my very closest friends, with whom I had spent many Christmas Eves in Houston, had died from complications of AIDS. His lover, whom I had never met or spoken with, was kind enough to go through "the little black book" to find phone numbers of friends he knew must be called. My friend of eighteen years and I had met in 1972, when he moved to Texas to work as an interior designer at the same place as I. It was long before AIDS came along, and we had had a tremendous amount of fun throughout the years. After he left Texas, he had moved to two or three other states before he settled in Kansas, and we were out of touch with one another until his HIV diagnosis. At that time, he was living in North Carolina, and called me to ask a lot of questions about Gary and AIDS. He had become part of a study at Duke

University in Durham, and made frequent trips to Mexico, where he had access to medications he could not afford in his city of residence.

Our subsequent phone conversations brought back many memories of the holiday dinners he had prepared for his mother and me before we went off to midnight mass, where he was the church organist. Most of those years he played the organ for the services, but one Christmas he had his own harpsichord taken to the church, so he could play music written for that instrument.

The day after the sad phone call from Kansas City, Gary and I met in the Tucson airport and flew together to Guaymas, Mexico. At the airport, we accepted a ride in a pickup truck from some locals whom we assumed earned money by taking travelers from the airport to their destinations. Looking back, I cannot believe we agreed to what could have been a risky decision. I was given the place of honor, inside the cab, while Gary rode in the bed of the truck with our luggage. Were we crazy? Apparently not. The driver, after stopping along the way to drop off one of his friends who had ridden in the back with Gary, took us all the way to the front entrance gate of Club Med—and then refused any payment from us. We were off to a good start.

The choice of Club Med was one that Gary felt would meet his need to relax, without having to drive from one motel to another. Nor would he have to endure traveling to and from restaurants. He definitely had to slow down and take care of his health. He wanted a vacation where he could stay in one place, and be away from the bustle of San Francisco and his daily commute over the Bay Bridge to Berkeley. Sometimes he rode the BART trains, but there was always the search for a parking space at the station, so this getaway would be just what he needed. There were no vehicles in sight on the premises.

The accommodations were excellent, with lovely rooms, mountains of food, nonstop activities, and nightly entertainment provided by the same people who worked so hard during the day to see to it that the guests were completely satisfied. Each night, after the shows ended and the "gentle guests," as were we called, retired to their rooms, the staff rehearsed their parts for the next night's show. I couldn't imagine where all their energy came from, but they were young, beautiful, and enthusiastic.

Before our vacation was over, Gary took scuba diving lessons and received certification. We rode horses, which for me was a new and exciting first. Ever so gently and carefully, the horses made their way through a large sandy field of cacti to the water's edge. As we galloped along the shore, I couldn't help but feel the exhilaration of sharing such an experience with my son. I never knew when it might be the last.

We had a wonderful time at Club Med and Gary's health was fine. However, when he cut his foot in the swimming pool, he felt obligated to inform the doctor who treated him of his HIV status, and was concerned that it might have some unpleasant ramifications. But it turned out to not be a problem.

Apparently, the trip was tiring for Gary. As we waited for our respective connecting flights in Tucson—Gary's to San Francisco and mine back home—he stretched out full-length on a bench in the airport, put his sleep mask over his eyes, and slept. That was the first of many such naps I would observe during our subsequent times together.

Little did I know at the time what was in store for Ken the very next month. I felt the maze closing in around me.

1990

35.
Ken

Yes. The same Ken.

Through all the years of my involvement, and even though we had begun to see that AIDS Foundation employees and volunteers were not exempt from HIV, it was a given that none of our invincible group would become a *them*. Remember, it was *us* and *them*. *We* had to take care of *them*. One fine day in September 1988, Ken called to let me in on his secret: he, too, was HIV-positive. Wait a minute! That wasn't sticking to the rules. Yet, why should I have expected that he would be excluded?

What was frightening to me was to realize that I wasn't shocked or frantic. Oh, no! I was becoming hardened! After all, we had already been in this thing for more than six years, and a cure would be coming any day. And besides, he wouldn't die from this. He still went about his business with me, and with all of the people whose health he monitored by phone on a daily basis. I became witness to this every Friday night, as I waited in his living room after work to go to dinner at our usual hangout, until I met the Michaels. And, as with Steve, I waited, and waited. Waiting included more drinks, though not for me. I should have seen the signs, but I had other missions to accomplish. Eventually, we would get to the restaurant and order more drinks, of course.

Life went on this way until one Friday evening early in

June 1990, after Gary and I had returned from Mexico. I arrived at Ken's condo complex before he got home from work, and was waiting for him in the parking lot. As he got out of his car and approached mine, I couldn't help but notice the orange tint of his face. It obviously was not a suntan, but against his impeccably tailored gray suit, it looked pretty darned good. He declared that he was not up to going out that night.

"I think I'll just stay in and try to get some rest. In fact, I think I'll go to bed."

And so began Ken's fight to the finish. A few days later, he called and said that he would be taking a few days off from work. Those rich ladies would have to do without him for a while. The next week didn't bring him any relief. He was exhausted and didn't know why. His latest charge, Brad, whom Ken had taken under his wing and into his house, had been difficult to care for. Brad's mother had given Ken the use of her car, which was supposed to be a good thing, but the purpose of her generosity was so Ken could take care of her son. Poor Brad. He suffered diarrhea in the car, he suffered it in the restaurant, and he suffered in general. But Ken was there, cleaning up and picking up after Brad. During one grocery shopping day, as I trailed behind him in the Disco Kroger, Ken muttered that Brad insisted on white bread, which Ken referred to as wallpaper paste. I haven't eaten white bread since.

The two of them, under one roof, were headed down a path from which there was no return. One week after another, Ken announced that he would go back to work the following week—and week after week, he didn't. What he was dealing with was a severe case of jaundice. As I recall, it was Ken's decision to check himself into the hospital and, at the same time, check Brad in as well. The plan was to achieve separation from Brad, who by this time was really getting on Ken's nerves.

Again, poor Brad. It wasn't his fault. Ken just couldn't keep up with the ever-increasing, self-imposed demands he had placed on himself. The hospital personnel were to place Brad in one wing and Ken in the other. Ken needed to be out of touch with Brad for a while, and with Brad's being in the hospital, Ken knew he would be well taken care of. It was a good idea until the second night, when Ken told me that Brad had phoned him in his room. I asked how Brad had found him.

"Easy," he said, "he just called the hospital switchboard operator." Oh, well.

The hospital had nine floors, with the patients' rooms arranged into three circular pods, or wings, on each floor. The nurses' station was at the center core of each pod. There were always so many patients on the AIDS floor that when we visited one person, we inevitably ran into other people we knew. It was like an ongoing party, except we weren't having any fun.

The nursing staff was quite open to providing information about their patients to just about anyone who asked. The AIDS community had become such regular fixtures around there that no questions were asked of us as to our credentials or our relationship to the patients. I think they needed all the help they could get.

There we were, four weeks after he had entered the hospital, with things not getting any better for Ken. He informed me that he was now receiving AIDS drugs. That would have meant drugs for a particular infection or illness that arose as a result of one's compromised immune system. There were no drug cocktails specifically designed to improve the immune system at the time. No one had told us that he had any specific infection. With Ken's latest announcement arousing my concern, I asked the nurse responsible for his care.

"Does he drink?" she asked.

"Yes," I replied.

"He ain't getting no AIDS drugs. His liver is telling on him."

What great news! They'll cure him of his jaundice, he'll give up drinking, and we'll all go back to where we were before he turned orange.

But it was the middle of July by then, and nobody was going anywhere. Brad was still there, calling Ken and coming by to visit, as were Michael B., Michael D., and I.

Time moved on and Ken's health wasn't improving. But I must have been functioning within a very strong denial system because I just wasn't getting it. He had to get out of the hospital and get back to work. Come on, Ken. What's going on?

Summer was in full swing and Ken was still in the hospital. I didn't have any idea what the doctors were doing for him. Before we knew it, it was Ken's birthday—the last day of August, reminding me of the big party he had thrown for himself in 1984, the one Fred didn't attend because he chose to die on that day, as Ken had said six years before. His favorite dessert was rhubarb pie, which he ordered every time we went to our usual Friday night restaurant. It was prepared by the hostess, whose son had AIDS. It seemed like the perfect "birthday cake," that rhubarb pie. So that was what I got for him, without the birthday candles.

Visiting other people in the hospital had been a lot easier—if there is such a thing—than what seemed like making small talk with Ken. He was usually an outspoken, dynamic guy who took control of nearly all of the conversation. Now he was weak; especially so, it seemed to me. When I asked if he wanted me to read to him, he definitely wanted to keep up with what was going on in the world. It felt strange reading to this man who was so independent and had been such a take-charge kind of person. But now that he could no longer do it himself, he still wanted to hear the latest news from *Newsweek* badly enough to have me read to him. I didn't like the feeling, but I read anyway. It was my realization of his vulnerability.

It struck me as odd the night of Ken's birthday that he was so cranky. When I noted that it was very cold in the room, he snapped at me, "Then go adjust the air conditioner."

His demeanor had changed. He was no longer the gentle man I had known, and it scared me. It was an all too familiar sign of worse things to come.

This was happening more than two years before Michael B. died. Both Michaels and I stood outside the hospital that Friday night and talked about what we would do the next day. I had left Ken deciding that I would not go to the hospital for his birthday because I assumed that he would have a lot of company; that many of his friends would be there with birthday wishes and balloons. It turned out that only Michael B. visited Ken on Saturday, not the horde of friends I had expected. The other Michael had not gotten as involved with the whole AIDS thing, in spite of his lover's health status.

That afternoon, I received a call from Michael B. that came as a complete shock. Ken had told him that he was tired and was going to take a nap. Michael assured Ken that he would be right there, just keeping him company, and not to worry about making conversation. But Ken never woke up. That was it. He was gone. Presumably a peaceful death. The only problem was that he wasn't supposed to die, for God's sake.

I don't know who called his family. I was flummoxed. Of course, by Monday we had things under control, with Ken's daughter, Jennifer, having arrived, and his ex-wife on her way, with their son, for a memorial service. Jennifer asked me to help her write the obituary. That was something new to me, but we did it. Including her mother as Ken's best friend, as he had described their relationship to me when we first met more than seven years before, was not well received by Ken's former wife, so we changed it. Jennifer asked me who might perform the memorial service. The only person I could think of was the same clergyman who had orchestrated Fred's going-away party, and he agreed to officiate.

On the way to the chapel, Jennifer's mother commented to me that she felt it was very unfair that the laws didn't allow gays to marry one another. I was glad to hear such a progressive view; I thought she was sympathetic to the cause. But she clarified it by saying that if they could marry each other, then some of them wouldn't feel compelled to live their lives masquerading in marriages, to the detriment and pain of others—meaning the families they created. In either case, I agreed with her, but we both had to admit that having those children was a good thing. And Ken had been devoted to them. I was disappointed that she didn't feel her relationship with him was the same as how he had described it to me. From Ken's positive description—that they were best friends—I was disappointed and saddened when she insisted that she hadn't felt the same.

The service was held at a chapel on the campus of a small, private university in the predominantly gay neighborhood. It is known for its meditative ambience and somber lighting on dismal paintings by Mark Rothko, for whom the chapel was named. I had never seen so many people in the place, where the only seating was a series of long, backless benches. Many people at the memorial service were Ken's customers, the wealthy ones whom he had served so well, and others were his coworkers, in addition to his associates from the AIDS Foundation. Still others were the many friends he had accumulated by networking in the AIDS community.

Of course, after the service, the closely knit group of friends—including Truman, the Michaels couple, Michael the pharmacist (whom I had called the night therapist Gary died), yet another Michael whom I had not met before, and Ken's family—met at the same restaurant I've mentioned so many times, the automatic pilot destination where we had continuously run into people Ken knew. It was fitting and proper for Ken. He owned the place that day.

The next day, Jennifer and I met at Ken's house to clean it out. There were multiple men's watches, which she offered to me, (I declined) and so very many books. She didn't want to deal with sorting them, so she just loaded them into boxes and put them out near Ken's parking place at the curb in the apartment complex. I could understand the reason for her haste in disposing of things, but it bothered me to see the books out there. The theory was that people would come along and take what they wanted, which would be a good thing. With that justification in mind, I retrieved the huge, hardback copy of *Lonesome Dove* that Ken had brought to me in the hospital (for a two-day stay) in 1986, and *Lincoln,* the Gore Vidal book I had given to Rick for his birthday in 1985. I'm glad I did, although I have not read either book. I just hoped it didn't rain before the rest of the books found new homes.

In the kitchen, there was a bay window with glass shelves displaying Ken's collection of knickknacks, among which was a yellow glass oil and vinegar cruet set I had brought to him from Israel in 1984, when Gary and I went to Egypt. I asked Jennifer to keep that as a remembrance of me, which was immediately reciprocated by her offering me a large, dark brown, ceramic coffee mug she had made and signed for her dad. That exchange was a tender moment for me.

We proceeded to the master bedroom to sort through

Ken's things. I knew Ken had been looking after a lot of people, but I had no idea I would find a stash of drugs he had been recycling from one person to another. If someone died or their medical protocol had been revised, Ken kept track of it all. His dresser drawer was a miniature pharmacy, full of all kinds of things, including everything from the most controlled substances to baby powder.

Jennifer and I boxed them up, and the following week I spent an evening with Michael, the pharmacist who had dispensed most of the meds the first time around to the people whose names were on the labels. I don't know if he knew that Ken had been giving the prescription drugs to people who needed them—a felony in the state of Texas—but he didn't seem to be alarmed. The drugs were very expensive and Ken didn't want them to go to waste, even though he knew he was committing a criminal act. We carried the large cardboard box to the kitchen sink, and Michael had me set aside anything he thought could be passed along, but very legally tossed the prohibited substances down the disposal. I was very proud to be associated with him in this activity, because he was obeying the law and I respected him for that. Of course, he also knew the penalty for not doing so. I could be trusted to keep it to myself, but how could he be sure of that? He simply did the right thing.

It was quite different from other evenings Michael and I had spent together in the past; putting up his Christmas tree, hanging ornaments, drinking wine while watching *Beaches,* and listening to Barbra Streisand records. It was tough.

After seventeen years, I still have the baby powder.

1990

36.
Brad

Most of what the Michaels couple and I knew about Brad had been learned from the experiences Ken told us about, but we felt an obligation to continue to visit him in the hospital. Of course, he was unable to attend Ken's memorial service. It wasn't long after a few of those visits that Michael B. informed me of Brad's untimely death at the age of twenty-nine.

Even though we had mixed feelings for Brad's mother, a woman who gave the care of her son over to another person, she was still a mother who had lost her son and I was very protective of that position. There was a good-sized group of people at the funeral home for the viewing of Brad in his open casket. Brad's mother, apparently to soothe her sorrows, exclaimed to the two Michaels and me, "Look at him. Doesn't he look good?"

What could we do but agree with her? Frankly, he *did* look good, but as Michael B. whispered quietly to me, "Yes, but he's dead."

It wasn't funny, but at the same time, all of us were becoming weary of the hold AIDS had on us.

1990

37.
Down Memory Lane

Carol, now my therapist for only eight months, had suggested that I join an AIDS support group led by Annette, a professional associate of hers. Groups such as this were in short supply in the city, but had been organized to allow people whose loved ones were ill to come together and discuss their mutual sorrows and concerns—not the least of which was the fact that they knew death from AIDS was inevitable. There was also still plenty of fear and prejudice from the general population to go around, which gave the group members all the more to share with each other. It was comforting to meet others who were experiencing many of the same fears as I. Actually, I already had six years under my belt, and was able to offer more experience to the group than I was receiving. But I was glad to be among people who understood my plight. I looked forward to our weekly meetings. But in time, Annette had other professional duties to attend to, and the group disbanded.

By the end of 1990, with Carol still trying to help me assuage my feelings of helplessness and hopelessness, she thought it might be helpful to bring Annette back to me for a short one-on-one connection. The day of our meeting, I had brought with me the Polaroid snapshot, a moment in time, which Joe had taken on my birthday almost six years before. There we were: Ken, Steve, Joe, his lover Tim, and myself, fluffy dog in my lap, all beaming at the camera, so very unaware at the time of what was to come. That is, we knew what was to come; we just didn't know how or when. Annette held out the picture, facing me, and asked, "What would Ken say to you if he were here?"

"I don't know," I replied.

"What would Steve say?"

"I don't know."

She continued in this way, naming each of the men in the picture. I didn't know why she was asking the question. All I could think of was, "How does she know their names?" I didn't have the presence of mind to realize that she had been reading their names, which I had written on the back of the photo in 1985. I *did* have the presence of mind to realize they were all dead.

1990

38.
Hawaii

It had been a year since I had last seen Gary, when we went to Club Med in Mexico. This year's vacation would be a biggie, all the way to Hawaii. Gary was feeling well, but I was concerned about how much weight he had lost in the past year. He had been steady in his resolve to continue his ballet classes and had developed quite muscular legs, but this year, they were very thin. I hesitated to ask questions and he didn't volunteer information, so we moved quite gingerly through our time together that beautiful week in June 1991, on the islands of Oahu and Hawaii.

We went to the usual tourist sights. At Hanauma Bay, we waded into the water and fed frozen peas to the spectacularly colored fish, which looked as if they had been designed and painted by someone under the influence of psychedelic drugs. One particularly memorable site was the Byodo-in Temple, set beneath the Koolau Ridge in the Valley of the Temples Memorial Park near Konehe. Inside the temple is an immense golden figure of Buddha, which in itself is quite impressive. But the serenity and inner peace of this splendid spot comes from the beauty of the temple and the exquisite gardens surrounding it. In an incredible Kodak moment, I was able to capture an image on film of the temple with the magnificent fog-enshrouded mountains in the distant background. I enlarged and framed a copy for Gary, and it is now a treasure for me to hold as I remember those most precious of moments together with him.

On the Big Island, we traveled the Chain of Craters Road determined to see the largest crater on the island. After stopping along the rim of what we thought was *the one*, and walking across the cooled lava flow of the still-erupting Kilauea Volcano, we returned to our car to check the brochure the ranger had given us *after* we had been to those places. It was then that we learned we hadn't seen Halemaʻumaʻu, the "really big one," which is about 3,000 feet across and nearly 300 feet deep. But it would have to do; it was getting dark, and we had to drive back to the western side of the island.

On the late-night drive back to our hotel, we couldn't help but notice how brightly the stars shone against the midnight black sky. Pulling off to the side of the road, we stepped out of the car into the cold, crisp air and gazed at the stars, sensing the bond we shared—just as we had done when we nudged each other upon hearing the exquisite chords of Richard Strauss' opera *Salome,* at a performance we had attended many years before.

My son and I used to share what we referred to as "peaks of joy" when we experienced a very special event together. One of these peaks of joy occurred the night we simultaneously shared the beauty of the full moon—although at the time, he was in his house in California and I was in mine in Texas. We were so very much of a like mind spiritually and emotionally that we had an innate way of connecting our souls, even when we were miles apart.

Without sharing every specific experience, each of which is indelibly etched in my mind, my purpose here is to create a path to the inevitable end of the memories of every glorious experience I was privileged to share with my son, knowing as they moved through our lives that each of them might have been the last.

1991

39.
Yellowstone

As usual, Gary made all the arrangements for our travel plans. This year, 1992, we would be vacationing in the summer instead of our traditional Christmas holiday week. Taking the Rocky Mountain train tour across Canada sounded great, so Gary got all the information, which included departure times from each of the towns on the route to the next. Not being much of a morning person, my enthusiasm quickly dissipated. My response of, "I can't get up that early!" was met with, "Then you decide where you want to go and you make the plans."

Yikes, that hurt. Nevertheless, after agreeing upon going to Yellowstone National Park, Gary still made the arrangements.

It was late August, when the weather was so much better any place other than where I lived. I spent a few days with Gary in San Francisco before we departed for Denver for a connecting flight into Jackson Hole, Wyoming. The small commuter plane out of Denver seated nine people, in addition to the crew. And seated we were. The ceiling of the small craft was not high enough for even the shortest passenger to stand, nor were there any facilities on board. Fortunately, it was a short flight, but it seemed much longer as the twin-engine prop plane flew through extreme weather conditions; lightning accompanied by heavy rain. Just to make things more interesting, my luggage didn't arrive with us, so a lot of time was spent on the telephone with the airline and the tiny airport in Jackson Hole.

Off we went to the town square of Jackson Hole, where the entrance at each corner of the block is arched with elk antlers picked up in the surrounding wooded areas by local Boy Scouts.

The next day was spent sightseeing around the Grand Tetons. In Moose, Wyoming, we came across a one-room church whose center aisle lined up perfectly perpendicular to the large picture window behind the altar. Through the window was the real-life picture view of the Grand Teton Mountains. When we returned later in the day for another breathtaking view, it had completely changed into one in which the mountains were barely visible through the dense fog. We left our prayer requests at the door, where I hoped someone would connect with my intense prayer for my son's health. I didn't know whether to tell Gary of my prayer; not wanting to sound maudlin, I chose not to. One more regret when chastising myself for all of the shouldas, couldas, and didn'ts.

Before we drove to Yellowstone, we checked with the airline once more to find out if my luggage had arrived at the Jackson Hole airport. No, it hadn't. So we left, with the reassurance that it would be delivered to the lodge where we would be for the next four days.

I enjoyed "playing survivor", making do with the clothing I was wearing and the small toiletry kit the airline gave me. But Gary thought I was upset about it and became quite cranky on my behalf. It was revealing of his health status, which I tried, in an amateurish way, to monitor without letting him know. I watched his movements, how he carried himself, how he responded to me, and particularly, his disposition.

His naps became routine each day as we traveled through the park. At each stop, whether it was one of the lodges scattered throughout Yellowstone or out in the beauty of the open landscape, he began to require more and more downtime. But it never occurred without his first locating an exceptionally grand view for me to drink in while he slept. He had developed a method of falling asleep at will. He told me, "In my mind, I draw a magic circle around me and if anything tries to cross over the line into the circle, I push it back outside." So his brief naps were all he needed in order to recover his strength.

We beheld nature's beauty in the palette of the Fountain Paint Pots between the Midway and Lower Geyser Basin. One pool resembled an oversized, liquid morning glory, among other small pools of different colors, made so by the minerals they contained. Of course, Old Faithful was as it should have been—faithful. Its eruption was not precisely on time, according to the schedule posted in the adjacent lodge, but when it did erupt, the show lasted for about twenty minutes. At the Grand Canyon of the Yellowstone, where we spread our blanket for reading, rest, and relaxation, we encountered a wildlife preservation group encouraging visitors to vote their opinion of whether or not gray wolves should be reintroduced to the park. There were solid arguments on both sides of the issue, and the ayes carried some months later.

As we continued through the week of exciting things to see and do, it became apparent that my son was getting tired. Once again, I speculated about our future together.

1992

40.
Back to Tim in '92

By the time I had returned home from my trip to San Francisco in 1989, when Tim had told me he would spend more time with his new boyfriend, he had decided to move in with Dan on a temporary basis. That turned out to be a good move, but Tim had left many of his belongings at my house, in case their relationship didn't work out.

What had been enjoyable for Tim and me gravitated to a relationship that involved all three of us. We went to many places, mostly outdoors, enjoying nature.

After their trial period of living together, Tim and Dan decided to make it permanent. Dan was in the medical field, so that became very valuable as Tim's health began to decline. I began spending more time at their apartment, still enjoying our close friendship.

As Tim became more bedridden, steps had to be taken to meet his rising needs. Having no success at finding a suitable bell for Tim to ring if he needed assistance, and he couldn't speak out loud enough for us to hear him over the television, Dan purchased a noisemaker with options. The choices of sounds were "siren," "car honking," and some other obnoxious noise— which, under the circumstances, was an incongruous mixture of pathos and comedy. But when Tim made his selection for calling us to his aid, he wasn't laughing, and neither were we.

Many times when I visited Tim, he asked me to close

the bedroom door so we could be alone. I treasured that time with him. Once, much to my surprise, he asked me to get into the bed with him, to feel the closeness that we shared. That relationship and my feelings toward it were tested on the day I was asked to stay with Tim while his mother and Dan went to make arrangements for Tim's funeral. I didn't like my role that day, but I'm sure not any less than the three of them were feeling about their own. Tim's mother had come from out of state and was determined to stay until Tim took his last breath.

After Gary and I returned to San Francisco from our vacation to Yellowstone in 1992, I received a phone call from Dan. I was apprehensive hearing his voice, feeling a sense of dread. I knew why he was calling. It wasn't until he asked me to have Gary pick up another phone, so he could tell us both at the same time that Tim had passed away, that I remembered. Oh, my God, I thought, he was Gary's friend, too. I had been so absorbed in my own relationship with Tim that I'd almost forgotten how important he was to Gary.

Later, when I learned that Dan had asked Gary to accompany him to the Lone Cypress at Seventeen Mile Drive in Pebble Beach, where Tim had requested his ashes be spread, I felt the circle had become complete.

1992

41.

Grace

Today is March 14, 2006. Thirteen years ago on this date, many friends and a few family members of Gary's gathered in the rear of the nave at Grace Cathedral in San Francisco to walk the labyrinth, which was a woven wool tapestry replica of the thirteenth century design laid in the floor of Chartres Cathedral near Paris, France.

There are three stages of the walk. The first part, until you reach the center of the labyrinth, is *shedding*; a releasing, a letting go of the details of your life. It quiets the mind. The second part is when you reach the center. You may stay there as long as you like. It is a place of meditation, to receive what is there for you to receive. As you leave, following the same path out of the center as you came in on, you enter the third stage. This is joining God, your Higher Power, or the healing forces at work in the world. As you slowly walk the path through the labyrinth, it is a time for reflection and contemplation.

Gary's purpose for the gathering was to commemorate ten years of living with AIDS. He was celebrating his life for what had been considered, at the time, to be long-term survival with the illness. Walking the labyrinth provided the opportunity for him to share with his family and friends the comfort and spirituality it offered. In doing so, the mysterious winding path becomes a metaphor for our own spiritual journey. It becomes a mirror for where we are in our lives.

We had been to Grace before, mostly on New Year's Eve, to hear the glorious organ recitals which are presented annually at the cathedral. But on March 14, 1993, the building took on a completely different ambience and meaning for us. Gary had chartered the whole building for his invitees, and was fortunate to have the organist from the Dallas Symphony Orchestra play slow, dark, and somber music for the duration of the time it took the many participants to slowly walk the labyrinth and gather, or give, whatever meaning was inspired along their path. Originally, a friend of Gary's was going to play the organ, but coincidentally, the professional from Dallas was visiting Gary's friend at that time and he willingly agreed to play, which greatly enhanced the occasion.

Before the ceremony of walking the labyrinth, at which Gary welcomed each individual slowly and graciously to enter the path, he spoke to the assembly. He introduced the Greek myth of the Minotaur which resided within a labyrinth and was slain by Theseus. Gary's explanation used the Minotaur, a monster, as a metaphor for one's own demons, or fears, to be conquered. To walk the labyrinth and contemplate one's life, and how to find peace or come to terms with those dark shadows, was his message.

Unfortunately, before the guests had arrived, Reverend Artress, with whom Gary had made all the arrangements for our use of the cathedral, found fault with the way Gary was dressed. He wore a beautiful long, teal blue, robe-like garment he had had made especially for the occasion. A gold brooch depicting the sun, with rays extending from the outer edges, was pinned to the lapel. The brooch was met with derision as to its possibly subversive meaning; perhaps because the Reverend Artress was not pleased with the clothing some of Gary's guests were wearing. She asked Gary, "What does that brooch mean?"

"It's the sun, a symbol of life."

"Well! I don't like the way your friends are dressed, either. I will speak to the group before you begin," was her indignant response.

And so she did. She told them that their clothing was not appropriate for a Christian church and that they were to remove those garments.

"But don't get naked."

What could they do? That was how they had arrived at Grace, and they were there for a good purpose. Many of them were Wiccan, and their garments were not exactly what you would see on an ordinary Sunday at Grace. But, come on! This was San Francisco.

One of my nieces, a Buddhist, had even sacrificed a gathering that afternoon which would have put her in the company of the Dalai Lama. Gary's celebration of his long-term survival was that important to her.

While he spoke, Gary had intended to have near him a bowl of water with a red rose floating in it, also as a symbol of life. He sadly decided to not display the rose, for fear of more criticism from Reverend Artress.

After everyone else had completed their walk, Gary entered the labyrinth, and I watched him move slowly along its path and wondered to myself what was going through his mind. I was to learn that afterward, on the way from Grace Cathedral to Gary's home.

He told me about the confrontation he had had before his celebration began, but he was not willing to share any more about it until he had taken a long nap after we returned to his house. He had been on the verge of heartbreak, but was determined to battle those feelings and had impassively shut them out during his walk.

The day before, we had driven to Berkeley to pick up a huge cake Gary had ordered for the reception the next day. When the friendly bakery shop clerk asked him what the occasion was for such a large cake, he told her of his celebration. She countered with, "My mother died of AIDS."

At that, Gary invited her to attend the ceremony, but she had to work. When we left the shop, we looked at each other and both said, "Did she say 'mother'?"

"Yes, she said 'mother'."

And the next morning, Sunday, March 14, he had gotten up early to go to the farmers market to buy two large flats of fresh strawberries for the reception after the labyrinth walk. As we sat together at the table cutting them up, Gary was excited about the day, and I was, as usual, extremely proud of my son for his positive attitude and joy in sharing it with others.

Now, after he told me of the disruption of his plans, I cried with him and we held each other close. It was a reminder of the New Year's Eve party he had prepared for a few friends when he was a teenager and nobody came. Only this time, learning from his experience of inviting only a few people, he had invited over sixty, many of whom showed up. Still, he once again had to deal with the disappointment of plans gone awry.

Gary worked to settle the matter by corresponding with Reverend Artress, who had upset his special day, until he was satisfied that they had come to some sort of peace with it. The irony of the confrontation and the story of the Minotaur was brought to a conclusion.

1993

42.
Camping Out

*A*ugust 18, 1993. Northern California Oracle Users Group awards Gary S. Wagman a Certificate for Contributions to his Peers in the User Group through Excellence in Publication of Originally Developed and Skillfully Executed Professional Materials.*

He was very proud of being honored for his work, as was I. He was also delighted to have been given a cash award as well. His original two-year contract with Lawrence Berkeley Laboratory had been extended four times. I was later told by his supervisor that he had a lifetime position there, which was meant to be for many years to come.

Our vacation the next month was a camping trip north of San Francisco, into the forest near the little town of Denny. On the way, Gary and I were very tired and made a short stop to spread out our blanket for some much-needed rest. By this time, Gary's need for restorative naps had increased, and I was quite willing to join him during a roadside stop along the way. It was such a peaceful time with my son, to be out in the crisp September air of northern California with what seemed like not a care in the world. In no time at all, I was sound asleep. When I awoke, Gary offered me wild blackberries that he had picked while I napped. It was such a simple gesture, but it reminded me of what a loving and generous child he had always been. He must have remembered that we had picked wild blackberries in Texas along the railroad tracks every chance we had when he was a youngster.

We proceeded to our campsite high above a crystal clear stream, and set up our tents. I had never been camping before, so it was a learning experience for me. The only signs of civilization were two outhouses and a water spigot. By the time we inflated our air mattresses, it was time for another nap for Gary. While he slept, I read *The Bridges of Madison County,* which I had been saving for this very occasion, and I had no trouble settling in for our stay in the peaceful outdoors.

Our dining needs were well met. Gary had brought fully cooked and frozen gourmet meals, which he had prepared a few days before we set out from his house. We certainly weren't roughing it.

I wanted very badly to talk with him about his health status. There were no phones or doorbells to interrupt us, but even though he assured me that I could ask anything I wanted to, I couldn't bring myself to spoil the lovely atmosphere we had made for ourselves out there in the woods. He still wasn't volunteering any information. I would have to monitor his health by observation and instinct.

I thought about the time, years before, when Gary had taken me out for an early dinner on the last Mother's Day we spent together. Afterwards, we drove to one of the large parks in Houston, where there was a pagoda-styled gazebo. Leaning against the railing provided a splendid view in all directions of the park and the people enjoying it on that beautiful May afternoon. I noticed a man, probably in his midforties, with an older woman I presumed was his mother. I turned to Gary and commented, "Look, there's someone else taking his mother out for Mother's Day. Did it ever occur to you that you might be taking care of me in my old age?"

"No," he replied. "I have been wondering who would take care of me in mine."

Who knew how the fates would turn? Who knew there would be no old age for him, and how often—particularly every Mother's Day—that incident would come back to me as a bleak reminder? Yet, he persisted in protecting me from what might become my ultimate challenge; that of providing the intimate care of my own son—for which I had, by then, an abundance of experience.

After dinner, we sat by the campfire waving the sticks we had lighted and pretended we were twirling lassoes with pinpoints of firelight. During the night, I became aware of how terribly hard the mattress was, but in the morning found that it was actually the ground under me because all the air had escaped from the mattress. Fortunately, there was a repair kit attached.

Another thing we found in the morning was that, even though we had packed all of the food carefully in the car, hoping to prevent visits from unwelcome bears or other critters, apparently it wasn't packed well enough. We did, indeed, have a visitor during the night as we slept so close to the action. Our private little campground was strewn with remnants which looked vaguely like what we had discarded from our dinner the night before. We could only speculate what creature had found our leftovers so appealing, but we knew we had to be more careful the next night.

The details of that trip are just as clear today as they were fourteen years ago, because every moment with my son was a bittersweet marker on the timeline of our relationship.

1993

43.

The Pinnacles

Upon arriving back in San Francisco from our camping trip, we were greeted by one of Gary's friends who asked how I liked camping out. I believe she was surprised to hear me effusively tell how much I enjoyed it—that it was an activity which had appealed to me for much of my life.

"Oh, really?" Her tone of voice and body language belied her response. I strongly sensed she was not happy to hear that. She and Gary had camped together before, and she appeared to resent that I had taken him away from her.

We had barely begun to take our camping gear into the house when she insisted that we leave the next day, Saturday, for a weekend at Pinnacles National Monument. It was one of Gary's favorite places of peace, spirituality, and connectedness to his Beloved, as God is referred to in Sufi literature. This is the place where he wanted his ashes spread.

Although he was incredibly tired from driving on the long trip back from our campout, Gary hesitatingly agreed. Once again, we were on the road, but fortunately his friend did the driving while Gary rested, as a passenger with me, in the backseat of his car. Jerry, another of Gary's friends, came with us and rode in the front. I was glad to have Gary to myself for a while.

There is more than one way to reach the top of the Pinnacles. They all are long and steep climbs, and Gary's choice—along with Jerry—was to take the most difficult of the paths. In order to begin the climb on the route they chose, hikers must enter the initial area from the parking lot by going through a very dark cave filled with large boulders, which must be strategically negotiated with careful footing and a good flashlight. Some of the boulders were so large and spaced so far apart, my legs could not reach from one rock to another. Sometimes Gary would help me by going ahead, then turning back to pull me by the hand. When necessary, he would get behind me and push to give me the forward motion I needed to climb to the next boulder. After the four of us made our way through the cave, Gary's aggressive female friend—who had demanded that we go to the Pinnacles—insisted that I stay back with her. I was not comfortable having to spend the day alone with her, especially after her response the previous day about my enjoyment of camping with Gary. We walked quite a distance through the grounds for about an hour, and now had the long hike ahead of us to return to the parking lot.

I asked, "Isn't there any other way to get to the car, without going through the cave?"

There wasn't.

As we neared the boulder-filled cave once more, close to the end of our route, we spied a huge tarantula, which interested her, but I needed to put some space between it and myself.

When she finished inspecting the spider, the first words she spoke to me were, "If Gary gets sick, are you going to come out here?"

"Of course," I replied.

"Well, you know he is sick now!"

That was swell! My knees began to tremble and I became

short of breath in response to what I had just heard. There was the cave just ahead of us through which we had to navigate, without Gary's help and encouragement, in order to get to the parking lot. I survived the strenuous ordeal, but my anxiety was soaring.

No, I didn't know that Gary was sick now, and I wanted him to be at my side right then. He had not been exhibiting any signs of illness, nor had he told me of any. It was getting late in the day and I wanted him safe, back down on level ground. As daylight faded and the moon rose, there was no sign of Gary and Jerry. I was highly agitated and sick with worry because I was filled with a strange, miserable emptiness. It was as if he had already left this earth for good, and I would never see him again. The feeling wasn't that he had died in the mountains. It was a sense that he had passed prior to then, and I hadn't been with him. I simply had to have him back to complete our life together the way it was ordained. It was difficult enough to know I was losing him to AIDS, and I couldn't imagine how anyone could bear the sudden loss of a loved one taken from them by accident or violence.

Had it not been for the light of the full moon that night, the two men would have had only a small beam of light from their flashlight to find their way down the dangerous, narrow path. But before they did, the person I was with ordered me to wait in the parking lot while she headed up the mountain to look for Gary and Jerry. I was furious with her demeanor and very concerned about Gary's fate. Not long after she left me alone in the parking lot, the three of them returned, and I was anxious to have Gary to myself again in the backseat of the car.

On the ride back to San Francisco, Gary stretched his

legs out over mine and soothed my fears while I soothed his tired, aching legs. Once we were alone in his home, with Gary lying comfortably on his bed, I told him what had been related to me—at probably the most inopportune time—when with trembling legs, I had to crawl over and up and down the huge boulders in the cave immediately after being told how sick he was.

Gary became very indignant. He said, "I am not sick! I don't know why she told you that."

Well, that was a relief.

"But," he said, "if I am ever so sick or demented that I can't communicate any more, don't prop me up in front of a television set and leave me there by myself."

As he spoke, his hands reached out, palms down, then he raised them slowly as if to levitate his soul. "Play some beautiful music that is soothing and will carry me up."

At least for that night, I went to bed knowing that my son was still with me, and might be for a very long time.

1993

44.
England

So far, 1994 appeared to be much like the previous years as far as Gary's health was concerned. He was taking some medications by then, but I wasn't being kept apprised of what they were or what they were treating. He was still in the mode of not worrying me unless there was something to worry about. That would come soon enough, but in the meantime, we decided to take another major trip; this time to England. As usual, Gary made all the travel and hotel arrangements. It was wonderful to know that all I had to do was show up.

At the end of March, we met in Dallas for the long flight to London. I came prepared with sleeping aids for the overnight flight, and Gary made sure we both had pillows and blankets. It was noon when we landed at Gatwick Airport in London and we were exhausted. Because of a late arrival in London, the airline presented all the passengers on our flight with 10£ vouchers for a meal in the airport. It was much more than enough for lunch, so we each bought two portions and bagged the extras for snacks later in the day. Sitting on high stools at a fairly small, round table in the airport restaurant, Gary observed that the tabletops were made of a beautiful dark blue, glittery marble. He made an immediate decision that he would select the same material for the countertops he would soon be installing in the new bathroom he had designed and was having built in his house.

Gary's house was quite old, but it was a solid structure. When he first purchased it, he was determined to remodel the entire house, and he set out on the project beginning with the kitchen and the bathroom, which backed up to each other. It was an obvious choice to combine the two-room job because of plumbing considerations. I was not only amazed by his design skills, but his personal execution of the work was also incredible, considering that he had never done that type of work before. Learning that he had also installed sheetrock, electrical fixtures, and everything else that goes into that type of construction, I asked where he learned to do those things. His response, "I read *Time-Life* how-to books."

As time went by, Gary began more and more to take his lab work home from the office. It would save him drive time, gasoline, and stress. By then, the computer system at the lab was networked so that working at home became a very distinct advantage. But the only place he could set up a workspace was in the cold, damp basement, which was not conducive to enjoying his job, in addition to not being good for his health. It was then that he decided to create two bedrooms and a bathroom downstairs, and an indoor staircase. He had also considered that I might have to stay for extended lengths of time if he became ill, so he provided this lovely environment for my comfort. While he expected to enjoy the new improvements to his home, he also accepted the fact that they would make the house easier to sell. It was for the new bathroom that the same granite as that of the tables in Gatwick was chosen.

Fortunately, the train station is within the airport terminal. We boarded the train to Victoria Station, where we would change trains to one which would put us near our hotel. Even after my trips with Gary to many foreign countries, I still enjoyed the feeling of navigating my way around new places. At Victoria Station, we lugged our heavy non-wheeled suitcases across the huge circular pavilion to the stairs leading to the platform, where we would board our connecting train to Paddington Station. There was no evidence of disability in Gary's stride or energy as he scaled the long, steep staircase ahead of me to the platform. As I slowly made my way up the stairs behind him, a polite gentleman coming down the stairs took my bag from my hand, carried it to the top, set it down, and turned and continued back down the stairs. I barely had a chance to thank him. What a wonderful welcome to London!

That afternoon, we fell across our beds into a deep sleep, from which we both awoke at the same time. We were totally in sync with each other, as usual. When we got our bearings, we went around the corner to an exceptionally good Chinese restaurant. As it turned out, that was probably the best meal we had during our whole trip through England and Wales.

The next morning we were off to Portobello Road, where we expected hordes of antique shoppers from around the world. Our first major mistake on this trip; the shops were closed the day we went, or we were in the wrong place. Still, that day we managed to squeeze in the British Museum, where Gary was intent on seeing the Rosetta Stone and the famous first-century Roman cameo glass Portland Vase. Of course, we visited St. Paul's Cathedral, Buckingham Palace, and the Tower of London, all of the usual touristy places. It seemed that we rode every line of the Tube, London's subway system, before the end of the day, leaving barely enough time to race to the Tate Gallery only forty minutes before it closed for the day. He just had to see the Pre-Raphaelites.

The next day was filled with equally impressive sights, among which was Hampton Court, Henry VIII's palace. We had lunch at a quaint little restaurant nearby with some friends of Gary's who lived in England, and got lost in the garden maze on the palace grounds. From that evening, when we picked up a rental car at the airport, we were on our own again—this time driving, for us, in uncharted territory. Exiting the airport parking lot and trying to enter traffic coming from the right took some adjusting on Gary's part, especially since we were turning left.

One of the highlights occurred as we approached Windsor. We were looking for a bed and breakfast where we could spend the night and be ready early in the morning for the tour of Windsor Castle. Driving past one possible place, we pressed on, thinking we might find a better one. But as our chances narrowed, we decided to go back to the B&B we had seen a few minutes before. Gary was becoming very tired, and we had to stop traveling as soon as possible. When we arrived at the inn we had passed a bit earlier, it was completely dark inside. I went in to see if there were any rooms available and was informed that the power had just gone off, from London to Windsor and parts beyond. The proprietor assured me that they could accommodate us for the evening, that he was able to prepare a fine meal for us on his gas stove, and he offered us free beer while we waited for the meal. We had a delightful candlelight meal in the otherwise dark dining room. There wasn't much else to do after dinner. So, finding our way up the winding staircase by candlelight, we were welcome to any room we wanted. As we lay on our beds talking in the flickering light, the ever present thought that *this* might be our last trip together once again flooded my mind.

By morning, the lights were on, and after an indulgent breakfast prepared by the proprietor, we were on our way to Windsor Castle. The guards were in full swing, and proved to us that it is impossible to make them smile, laugh, grimace, or otherwise show any indication that they are human, except for their continuous pacing and ordering tourists to "remain behind the line."

One of Gary's greatest desires was to visit the Royal Pavilion in Brighton. Plowing through the driving rain, we arrived late the night before Good Friday. There were no bed and breakfast rooms available because of the holiday, and finding a place to eat dinner was no easier. We were able to locate a hotel with a vacancy, but the only available parking was five blocks away. It wasn't until after we carried our luggage through the near-freezing rain, facing the wind blowing in from the sea, did we realize that we could have just taken from the car what we needed for the night.

Then we had to find a place to eat. The only place open was a hamburger joint across the street from the hotel. We were pretty desperate by then, although my appetite had vanished. Our conversation was about my family history and my personal problems. I was taking advantage of our being together to explain some of the reasons for what I perceived to be excuses for my many shortcomings as a mother. It was as if I had to let him know, while I could, that I wanted to apologize for every mistake I had ever made in his life. I suppose it was to assuage all the guilt feelings in one brief exchange, but I felt stifled and uncomfortable. It may have been because we were so far from home, or it might have been the storm. I had hoped that being together, away from our daily routines, would offer an opportunity for us to open up and express ourselves without any reservations. However, I sensed discomfort on Gary's part; which, in turn, didn't feel right for me and probably not for Gary, either. That would become a reality soon enough. Gary must have assumed that our agreement years ago of sharing our feelings extended from peaks of joy to valleys of sadness.

Even with double-paned glass in our eleventh floor room, we could still hear the wind howling outside. Then Gary announced, "I have something to tell you."

His phrasing struck me as ominous, but I didn't have long to wait before he continued. "My T-cells are gone. I didn't know when would be the right time to tell you. If I told you at the beginning of our trip, it might have spoiled it for you, but if I waited until the end, I would have felt that I had betrayed you by not being forthcoming."

My whole body began shaking uncontrollably. I sat on the edge of my bed, dumbstruck. Gary reached out his hand for me to go to him. When I did, we lay on his bed as he held me close. For God's sake, I was supposed to be comforting him. I didn't cry; I just kept shaking, and feeling horrible for spilling out my troubles at the same time he was contemplating how to tell me his unbearable news. How would we continue what we were doing there? How could we go on at all, anywhere? At least we were together when he told me, and I'm sure that was what he had in mind when he decided to wait until then.

Sleep did not come easily that night. But when morning arrived, a new and sunny day, we visited the pavilion, took pictures of each other, and passed the day as if nothing was wrong.

Before the trip was over, we visited Shakespeare's home in Stratford-on-Avon, Warwick Castle, drove through the well-known green expanse of the countryside in Wales, and pondered the mysteries of Stonehenge near Salisbury. We caught sight of the white horse painted on the side of the hill at Wiltshire, about which folklore and legends abound.

Gary wrote, "I prefer a vacation where I can stay in one place, but new territory always beckons rental cars into their grasp. We were not deterred by the typically British weather or the left-handed driving."

The bitterly cold wind and rain couldn't have kept us from attending Easter service at Wells Cathedral. Before we left our cozy room on the third floor of a 900-year-old hotel, we talked about the fact that we would be going home four days before his birthday. He had made no plans for observing it, but decided then that he would have a big party the next year.

Arriving at the cathedral in time for the sermon, we were surprised that its subject was the movie *Schindler's List*. It was delivered by the Canon and Precentor of Wells, Keeper of the Fabric, The Reverend P. de N. Lucas. I was impressed that he chose that movie for an Easter sermon, and when I returned home, I wrote to him to request a copy. It was sent to me with an apology for the last-minute corrections on the handwritten text. He explained that all of his sermons are handwritten, and it was comforting to me to know that there were times and places where computers did not belong. In closing the sermon, he claimed, "Giving is the real getting. Letting go is the true saving."

We were so taken with the sermon, the music, the parishioners, and the glorious beauty of Wells Cathedral that we returned for the evening service. Of course, there is always a gift shop, and I couldn't resist purchasing a tape of the Wells choir. For days to come, as we drove through the countryside of England and Wales, the voices from Wells filled our hearts. We both agreed that Wells was the highlight of our trip. But I knew that in the future whenever I played that tape, the images collected on that drive would forever conjure up the pain of knowing that *this was* the last vacation with my son.

1994

45.
Beginning of the End

The next several months were relatively uneventful for Gary, as far as I knew. By then, he was taking an assortment of prescription medications for some infections that began to creep into his life. He was still working full time at the lab, although he required daily naps on the egg-crate, foam-rubber mattress he had placed under his desk. When he informed me of his failing health, I remained in such denial that I'm afraid he must have thought I was insensitive. It wasn't as though I had never heard the same words from others. It had to have come from my refusal to accept the truth that AIDS is incurable, and that the time had come when my son would have to endure the misery that went along with it.

In September, a horrendous case of haemophilus flu took hold of Gary and wouldn't let go. His weakened immune system was unable to completely fight it off. Even after he recovered enough from the flu to return to work, he continued to cough incessantly. Once, while he was driving home from work across the Bay Bridge, he began coughing so hard that it caused him to vomit. There was no way to pull over to the side of the road. He was so sick, yet when he got home, he knew he had to clean the car before he could go into the house and fall into bed.

He continued his work at the lab, but by the time he got home in the evening, he was too tired to prepare dinner. So he enrolled in the meals-on-wheels program through Project

Open Hand, which provides nutrition services to people living with HIV/AIDS, other critical illnesses, and to seniors. Fortunately, he was able to pay for the service, even though it wasn't expected of him. Rejecting the possibility of retiring on disability status, Gary fought with determination to stay the course.

Spending Thanksgiving in San Jose with his cousins was very important to Gary, and was a holiday gathering he was not about to miss. So, with the help of a friend who drove him there, he managed to show up—but he was too sick to participate. Retiring upstairs to his cousin, Nancy's bed, he remained there until Nancy went upstairs for something. It was fortunate that she checked on him, because he was too weak to call out, much less go downstairs and announce his plight. He apparently knew that he was ill enough to require hospitalization, which would be the first since his diagnosis, eleven years before. In fact, his first since he was born. He had always been a healthy child, never missing a day of school. Now his temperature was 104.6°F.

My brother, Elliot, who had been there with his wife and children for the holiday, drove Gary to the hospital, with some of the family going along for support. I was informed that I'd better get to California as soon as I could. On Saturday, I arrived after midnight at my niece's house, very anxious to see Gary, but I had to wait until the next day.

When I got to the hospital, things were looking up and Gary was in high spirits, which would last for the next week or ten days. He was feeling better, apparently from some miracle treatment prescribed by his assigned doctor at the hospital. It is agonizing to me to know that when it came to my own son, his illness, and the care he received, I was not there, as I had been for so many others. One reason was that the others were in the city where I lived, and the other was that Gary persisted in his refusal to cause me any anxiety. Or perhaps it was my complete denial that my son could have a fatal illness—or worse, that he was very close to the end of his life. I pleaded with the nurse for any information about what I could personally do for my son. I offered a lung transplant, which she said was not possible. I told her, "I will give him a *life* transplant if it can be accomplished."

That was met with compassion, but of course, another rejection.

During his stay in O'Connor Hospital in San Jose, Gary wrote a letter to President Bill Clinton expressing his feelings of gratitude for all of the research and treatment afforded to AIDS patients. I was not permitted to read the letter, so I cannot say what Gary's purpose was in writing it, except that I believe he was very grateful for the care he had received, and was happy to be alive.

Gary later wrote to me, "...all in all, the hospitalization was not a bad experience. In fact, it was a very *moving* experience, as I understood the dedication of hundreds of thousands of people whose efforts were flowing into *my* arm day and night. Also, I was in a highly elevated spiritual state, and everyone listened to me and asked interesting questions without pushing themselves on me."

The following Wednesday, he literally danced his way out of the hospital for the ride back to San Francisco in his car, which had been left in San Jose for my use. The only problem was that the muffler had fallen off in the parking lot of the hospital on the day I had arrived. I tried to have it replaced at a dealership in San Jose before Gary was released from the hospital, but they were unable to accommodate me. It was the first time I had driven on California highways, and as we roared down the road, I was afraid of being stopped by the highway patrol. But that fear faded behind us, and was soon replaced by the ones ahead of us in San Francisco.

For the next two weeks, daily eight-hour intravenous infusions were administered to Gary, during which time he lost fifteen pounds and practically all the strength he had regained in San Jose. He tried to eat what I prepared for him, but the IV treatment seemed to be hurting more than it helped, causing persistent weakness and nausea. Yet, his steadfast resolve was to recover from what had apparently been his first bout of pneumocystis carinii pneumonia (PCP). Paul, the male nurse who arrived daily on his motorcycle, was a very handsome young man who encouraged Gary from the moment he came into our lives. His assignment was to administer the daily intravenous infusions of Pentamidine and Rocephin.

Gary referred to Paul as "nurse on a bike." I preferred "biker nurse". I assumed he was gay, but he was not. He expressed to me his concern for what was happening within the gay community regarding AIDS, and the bigotry that went with the territory. He worked with many gay men with AIDS, and had heard their stories of rejection from their families, their loss of jobs and friends, and in general, their loss of health and autonomy. When his two-week assignment was over, Gary gave him a generous monetary gift of thanks. Before he left Gary's house for the last time, Paul bent down to whisper his compassionate goodbye in Gary's ear.

December 17 was the anniversary of the death of Rumi, the founder of Sufism, and was to be observed with a huge gathering in Seattle. Rumi's followers call it the "wedding night"—that is, when Rumi was "married to eternal life." Gary had already purchased airline tickets for us to attend the sema, in which he was to participate in the turning ceremonies.

I didn't dare to ask him, as each day he became weaker, whether or not he felt that he would be able to take the trip, never mind participate in the program. But on December 16, he asked me to call the airline to cancel our reservations because he knew he was unable to go. He had fought the good fight, but hadn't won the war. However, he gratefully accepted the fact that he was improving, and planned his return to work after the New Year holiday. He rose to the occasion of attending the turning ceremony in Fairfax, California, across the bay, but was unable to complete the turning portion, when weakness gave way to preservation of his dignity. As he wrote on January 2, 1995, "My strength vanished in November along with my ability to fully participate in the annual celebration (the sema) of Rumi's passing. I was supposed to turn in the shortest segment (salam) of the ceremony, yet had decided that I was not strong enough. Then by a quirk of positioning, I found myself on the floor anyway. I marched to the sheikh, bowed, and spun to my place in the inner circle. However, I quickly discovered that I could not control my placement, so, using the grace of fifteen years of ballet training, turned right off the floor to the sidelines. I had to sit out the following two salam, which ceremonially, is considered bad form."

Yet, in the same letter, he wrote, "Many times when pondering Rumi, the 13th century founder of the Dervishes, I get a joyous, inspired feeling that does not compare with materially-based, temporal joy."

His perseverance to attend the sema and, even greater, his determination to do the best he could, considering his weak and tired body, filled me with pride and overwhelming sadness. Yet, he knew that the manner of his early departure from the floor, where his classmates had turned in all four salam, totaling forty-five minutes, would appear less obscure than it might have had he collapsed in the midst of the most important part of the ceremony.

The next day, Saturday, December 18, a call came from Project Open Hand asking if Gary would be home that day, as they wanted to bring a Christmas gift bag to him. Of course, it would be very welcome. As we sat on the dining room floor, I watched as Gary opened the ten or twelve packages. We both were overwhelmed with emotion. We had been volunteers before and had a sense of gratitude for our good fortune of not needing to depend on charity for our survival. We were overcome by the feeling of being on the other side of the fence.

Among the gifts were pictures drawn and colored by young children, who expressed their compassion and love with sweet messages that could break your heart. One exceptional drawing was of a horse. It was obvious that the young artist had a keen interest in horses, whether or not it had anything to do with Christmas. That was what made this particular gift so special; that this child shared his or her love with a total stranger in a manner which was particularly special to them.

Who were these children and how did they get involved? It brought us to tears.

We did manage a day out before I returned home. After seeing the movie *Priscilla, Queen of the Desert*, where Gary expressed his need for a donut cushion, we went out to eat at Max's, Gary's favorite diner, requested a takeout box for most of the food for the next day, and went home. He was exhausted.

At the end of each year, physicists from around the world

meet at the lab in Berkeley to review the accomplishments of the past year and discuss plans for the coming year. Gary had been assigned to make the presentation to the attendees. Preparing for the possibility of his inability to attend, he called a coworker to alert her that she might have to fill in for him. But the next day, it was fortunate that we had gone, because when we arrived at the lab, she was not there. Gary gave his presentation, assisted by Paul, not Gary's nurse, but the person who was hired to replace Gary after his imminent death. It was ironic that a few months before, when Gary informed his supervisor of his illness, he was told that he would be the one to interview and hire his own replacement. It was, to say the least, an uncomfortable task. But since he was the only person who knew his job so thoroughly, it was logical that he be the one to explain it to the applicants. He selected Paul as the most-qualified person and went about training him, even though no one knew exactly when he would have to take over Gary's job. Paul ran the slide projector during the presentation, while Gary stood before the group in his heavy winter jacket, feeling extremely cold and weak. As soon as his part was over, he was ready to leave. As we made a hasty retreat out the door, Paul followed us and thanked Gary for being so gracious.

While crossing the Bay Bridge back to the city, I asked Gary how he felt about knowing what Paul's role would become. His reply, although I'm sure understated, was, "Weird."

In his New Year's letter the next week, he wrote, "When I saw my blood counts (reds, platelets, whites, lymphocytes, neutrophils) drop, I decided to tell everyone at work and to ask for another programmer to be hired so that I could train them. The Physics Division agreed. Interviewing candidates to replace me and training the new hire seems like an absurd arrangement, but I asked for it because I felt that it would be fairest to the wonderful people I work with."

A few days later—weak, yet hopeful—Gary drove me to the airport and we said our goodbyes. I didn't want to leave, but I recalled that ten days earlier I had reminded him that his usual two-week limit for my visits had, this time, been extended to four. I knew how important his independence was to him.

"I know," he said, "but I really needed you." And this time, I *knew* that we would never be going anywhere together again.

1994

46.

No Red Roses

Monday, April 17, 1995. While at work, I received a call from the same woman who had insisted on going to the Pinnacles after my camping trip with Gary. She informed me that I'd "better get to San Francisco while he was still lucid." What a way to put it. What was that supposed to mean? I had just spoken with Gary a few days earlier about his planned trip here to join my family's reunion, arranged by my brother, Elliot, on the premise that my siblings were growing old and might never be able to see all of each other if we waited much longer. Gary had entered the hospital on his birthday, April 11, at the doctor's suggestion that they investigate more thoroughly why he wasn't feeling well. He had been in the hospital only once before, at the end of 1994. When I called him on his birthday, I left a message and expected a call in return. However, the call I received was not to acknowledge mine, but to let me know that he was in the hospital. My reaction was, "But it's your birthday."

And his was, "Yeah, bummer."

I recalled his comment the previous year on that rainy day in Wells, when he said he would have a big party this year. But that was not to be. From that day forward, I called every day until he suggested I discontinue doing so because he was too ill to speak. I wanted to go to San Francisco to be with him, but he insisted that I not come, as he was expecting to attend the reunion the following week. It was difficult to not call, but that was his request and I abided by it. Before that, in discussing whether or not he would be coming to the reunion, he said the doctor assured him every day that they would have to take it one day at a time. Then that phone call came. I had not been apprised of the details of his worsening condition. Why had no one called me before? And why might he not be lucid? Gary's friend had assumed the role of making decisions on his behalf without consulting me, as she had been instructed to do. She telephoned me at her own discretion.

The next day I was on my way to San Francisco, standing at the back of the plane for the duration of the flight. My stomach was in knots and it hurt to sit down. Three and a half hours later, I was whisked to the hospital. I found my son in good spirits and certainly not mentally compromised. My concern was well-founded, but also tempered with a somewhat cavalier attitude that he just needed to be treated for whatever his body was dealing with, and then I could take him home. That had happened the previous December. Just get better and let's get out of here.

By Wednesday morning, things were looking up. Gary asked me to call the secretary at his office so he could report the work hours he had accumulated up to the day before he entered the hospital. Then he wanted me to get some toothpaste for him to use with the electric toothbrush I had mailed to him as a birthday present, and find some kind of juice or nectar for him that didn't contain ascorbic acid. As I left the room, I paused, wanting to say, "I love you." But not wanting to sound maudlin, I went out, thinking to myself, You'll regret not saying it. But I didn't say it. And I *did* regret it.

I took my time, walking to the few neighborhood stores near the hospital, then down the hill to the big Safeway, all the while thinking that I was giving Gary some quiet time alone. When I returned, without having been successful in finding the right juice, Gary was sitting up in bed and brushing his teeth with water and no toothpaste. He hadn't wanted to wait for my return. Then we found the small tube of toothpaste taped to the bottom of the toothbrush charger, but he was too exhausted to go through the exercise again. After rinsing his mouth, he said, "Next time, don't stay away so long."

As I took a seat in the big chair next to his bed, once again thinking I was letting him get some much-needed rest, and recalling Michael's experience with Ken, I assured him that I would be there with him. But he didn't want that. He said, "Put your chair in front of the bed so I can see you."

These efforts on his part to bind us closer did not go unnoticed by me. They were different from our usual style of communication, and while I cherished them, they scared me. When he wiggled his toes, I thought he wanted the covers pulled up, as Art had indicated eleven years before. I asked if that was what he wanted, but Gary replied, "No, I was just waving hello."

Another thing that was noticeably different was that when Gary said he was bored, he decided to watch television, something he rarely did. He had never wanted to own a TV because it would have kept him from what he considered more productive pursuits, such as reading, working on his home remodeling, raising dahlias, and studying his Rosicrucian books or his Sufi material. As he flipped through the various cable channels, we noticed that many stations were reporting an explosion that had taken place in Oklahoma City.

Gary asked, "What is all this about?"

We weren't really paying close attention to the news from Oklahoma. At the time, neither of us realized the magnitude of the bombing of the Federal Building in Oklahoma City. Gary needed to find something entertaining. Just as he was settling on the movie *Sinbad*, a doctor came into the room to report that the medications Gary had been given were beginning to take effect. What a relief!

The rest of the afternoon and evening were spent receiving a few visitors and simply being together. His Sufi teachers, Halaal and Rashid, brought flower buds, chosen so that Gary could observe the process of their opening, which held the message of rebirth and the continuation of life. Halaal read poems by Rumi until Gary became too tired to listen anymore. I went out to dinner, reassured that Gary was going to be just fine. The hospital had provided a room for me to spend the night, and when it was time to leave Gary, I retired to my room with a book and a bag of cookies, as though I had nothing to worry about.

At 6:30 AM, Thursday morning, a call came from the nurses' station on the floor above mine. I was told that Gary had taken a turn for the worse. For God's sake, I didn't even know what was wrong with him in the first place! Why wasn't anybody telling me anything, and where was his primary doctor? Why was I so blasé, and why wasn't I asking questions? After all, for twelve years I had prepared myself for this. Apparently, I had retreated into a very deep sense of denial because the reality of the situation wasn't registering with me.

The first thing Gary said when I entered the room was, "Call Halaal for me."

I replied, "It's only seven o'clock."

"Just dial the number. I want to thank her for the flowers and the poetry."

Other than his voice sounding so terribly weak, it seemed to me that, with the right care, he would soon be better. Then we could go home.

I realized that, over the years, I had spent an enormous amount of emotional energy in my work as a volunteer, but suddenly I felt that the drama was gone. Only in retrospect could I see the situation in Davies Medical Center Hospital that week as carrying the same amount—or more—of the same intensity as I had been a part of so many times before. But at the time, I must have been defensively numb. It felt like I wasn't involved enough; and I wasn't. The hospital staff had no way of knowing that I was not only a well-informed and well-experienced AIDS worker, but also a very well-informed mother. At the time, I wasn't thinking about the politics of it all. Yet, I still didn't know what my son was suffering from. He just needed to get better and get out of there...but that, like his anticipated birthday party, also was not to be.

Thursday afternoon brought the first appearance of Gary's primary care physician since I had arrived. Only later did I realize, and regret that I had not been standing at Gary's bedside when the doctor informed him that there was nothing else he could do to save my son. He issued a choice for Gary to make: go on a ventilator, or be administered morphine. Gary had, for many years, been concerned about developing dementia and being unable to speak for himself. He had already made that quite clear the night we returned from the Pinnacles. Fortunately, that did not occur. So, with the ability to make his own dubious decision about the very short remainder of his life, he was very vocal about not being put on a ventilator.

I don't know if he was aware that the time he had left was so limited, but we didn't use it to say our goodbyes. By Friday morning, it was clear that he would soon be leaving. Yet, when a volunteer arrived to see if Gary wanted a back massage, the answer was yes. When I saw Gary struggling to turn over, I asked, "What do you need?"

"For the massage," he whispered.

I left the room so he could relax in the arms of the gentle man who had offered one of the most comforting of services.

When I returned, neither of us spoke of the inevitable end of our lives together. I couldn't tell him. I just wanted to crawl into the bed with him and hold him. Not wanting to make him uncomfortable, particularly since he was no longer speaking and unable to tell me whether or not he wanted that much closeness, I merely stood by his bed and sang softly to him, "Hush little baby, don't you cry." In a minor key. Where did that come from?

At one point, a nurse entered the room and announced, "Well, it won't be long now."

"Get her out of here," I demanded.

I couldn't believe her lack of sensitivity. Sure, she probably saw this scenario day after day, but I didn't. At least not with my own son, for God's sake. I never saw the staff or a doctor again.

Gary's half brother and his wife arrived that day. The three of them had only in recent years gotten close to each other, and it struck me as a scene from a soap opera—my meeting Gary's other relatives under those circumstances. Gary's sister-in-law volunteered to find her way to the San Francisco airport to pick up my brother, Elliot, who had left his family reunion chores to come to my side and to say goodbye to Gary. His arrival was a complete surprise to me.

One of Gary's cousins and a few friends were down the hall, for which I was grateful because I wanted to be alone with my son. It was midafternoon, and Gary lay breathing very heavily with an oxygen mask over his nose. There was no music, only the sound of the second hand of the clock on the wall ticking away the last precious moments.

Thinking of Bruce Davison's character in *Longtime Companion*, I repeated his line, "It's okay to let go." I didn't really want to say that, but Gary was struggling to breathe and it was all I could do to help him. Feeling that perhaps he might feel an expanse of time between my love messages to him, and that he might think he was alone, I occasionally reminded him that I was there. I told him, "I know this sounds silly, but, if you know that I'm here, can you blink for me?"

His eyes opened ever so slowly, then closed again. That was the best I could hope for. He knew. I wanted to get on the bed with him, but ever mindful of protocol, I refrained from that. At 4:15 PM, he lurched forward, and I thought, Oh my God, this is it! But it wasn't. I thought, He's still with me. Then again, and yet again, he came forward, opening his eyes, and then he was gone. I looked at the clock.

4:18 PM

I remembered what Brad's mother had said about her son, "Doesn't he look good?" It no longer seemed a ridiculous thing to say. I was fortunate that, in his repose, I had a beautiful image of Gary to carry forward with me for all time.

Some unknown force within me took over, and I went to the flower arrangement Halaal and Rashid had brought to Gary two nights before. The petals were now falling onto the table. I picked up several yellow tulip petals and placed them on the pillow in a semicircle over Gary's head.

Rashid and Halaal arrived later in the evening, and as the other people gathered in the room, Rashid and I performed the ritual cleansing of the body, after which Rashid dressed Gary in his Sufi turning garment and gently tucked Gary's sikke into the crook of his arm. I hadn't realized that Rashid had to have moved the petals in order to put the garment over Gary's head. Only when I looked up and saw him, without question or comment, replacing the petals precisely where they had been on the pillow, did I attach the symbolism of the yellow petals as a golden halo above my angel's head.

As we bent over Gary, the others in the room had been removing the medical supplies and everything that had been used to sustain his life until he took his last labored breath. By the time Rashid and I completed our tender task, the room had been transformed into a dimly lit, loving space. Gary was surrounded by the flowers Halaal had brought, now fully open, in addition to all of the other combined tokens of birthday wishes and get-well cards.

From the time Gary was a baby, before I tucked him in and kissed him goodnight, I would place my ear over his heart and listen to it beat. No matter how old he was, if I was with him when he went to sleep, the habit remained. Once, when he was living in New Orleans, I thought of him walking with long strides on Canal Street, and visualized that same heart beating somewhere in Louisiana. It didn't really matter that I couldn't put my head to his chest. It was the fact that the continuing life I helped bring into the world was out there, and I would someday be able to listen again. In the past, I had shared that thought with him. He understood me. Now, in Davies Medical Center, the memory surfaced, and I didn't dare to even think about it further.

It was agonizing to leave Gary for the last time. My son, my only child, the love of my life. He looked beautiful.

I placed a full yellow tulip over his heart and repeatedly kissed him until I knew that my brother and I had to go. The next day, walking with Elliot and Gary's half brother and his wife through Muir Woods, on the northern end of the Golden

Gate Bridge, I silently thought, Red roses are the symbol of love. Why did I not place a red rose on his breast?

Because there were no red roses. It was inevitable that the golden tulips were meant to be his halo, emanating his gift of light and life. And love.

Friday, April 21, 1995

RAM'S WEDDING

Light one,
Go to your Beloved.
Your seeking is over.
Merge with all the atoms
Of the Universe,
Embraced in the Heart
Of the One beyond our Naming.

The candle
That we lit for you
Kept waking me from sleep.
Calling me to think of you,
To pray and to remember.
In the night I saw your clear face,
Clasped your hands.

Light One,
Dance with your Beloved.
Go with God.
There is none but That
In which you spin now.
There always was no face
But That face.
Turn and kiss.

T. Thorn Coyle 4/22/95*

*Used with permission of the author.

AFTERWORD

L ife went on. I came back home to the family reunion. I even washed the windows I was planning to clean the day before Gary was to have arrived. I justified that apparently irrational action to my next-door neighbor. I was doing it as a symbolic gesture for Gary.

I drove to the airport to pick up or deliver people more times than I could count. There was no funeral or service for Gary, other than the recitation of the mourner's prayer at my family's reunion, led by my brother who had gone to California for Gary and me. On the airplane coming back home, three days after Gary died, Elliot wrote a touching tribute emphasizing Gary's intellect and excellent performance at his job, as praised by his peer group at Lawrence Berkeley Laboratory during a gathering at Rashid's and Halaal's home. He wrote of Gary's dedication to his search for enlightenment with the Sufi Order, and of his outstanding talent in the remodeling of his home. Five days later, he read this to the family at the reunion luncheon. I am forever indebted to Elliot for his demonstration of love and acceptance of my son. He passed away April 16, 2007, before having the opportunity to read this tribute to him.

October 8, 1995. My sister, Bea, went with me to California for the spreading of Gary's ashes at the Pinnacles. Because of the number of people who would have been unable to scale the rocks in the dark cave, as we had done in 1993, we took one of the alternate routes to the top. This time, I knew I had to climb the long, steep mountain to reach the place where we would cast my son's ashes to the universe. My other sister, Vivian, who could not attend, sent with me packets of flower seeds, including Texas bluebonnets, to spread the tiny beginnings of renewing life. I mixed them into the ashes so that wherever they may have fallen, they might bloom along the mountainsides.

Once again, at the Pinnacles, my role as Gary's mother was undermined by the same person I had been with the previous time. I asked her to give Gary's ashes to me so that I could carry them to the top of the mountain. Her refusal stunned me into irate silence. Bea hurried over to me, put her arm around me, and asked, "Why not?"

The answer was a loud and flat refusal. "Because!" she said, thrusting her arms quickly downward to her sides, like a stubborn child.

By then I was so shaken that I feared being unable to make the long climb. I was told by the keeper of Gary's ashes that I didn't have to go all the way to the top. I truly believe she did not want me to get there, because she had orchestrated the whole ceremony and considered me an outsider.

Bea and I stayed together during the arduous climb. At one place, we stopped and sat on a rock while, with her arm around me, she sang a lovely lullaby, "My Curly Headed Baby." Though I was sobbing, it was just what I needed to give me the strength to reach the top, as I felt Gary knew I would.

Once we reached the top of the mountain, I sat on the ground and ran my fingers through the small mound of ashes that had been placed there, together with a few mementos offered by some people in the group. My red ribbon was among them.

Halaal, Gary's Sufi teacher, began to do the traditional turning dance on the very edge of the high peak where we had gathered. We were literally at the pinnacle of The Pinnacles. As I looked up to watch Halaal, I noticed a black bird circling immediately overhead, very close to the assembled group. Bea and I felt an ominous foreshadowing in its presence. It was not an unfounded feeling, as the antagonism of the person whom Gary had called his friend continued for another five years, and has never been resolved. She made promises to him which were not kept, and she betrayed both Gary and me with her complete disregard for him. Gary felt that he had taken care of his earthly business by putting his trust in her, but she chose to betray that trust.

By October 1993, I had drifted away from the AIDS Foundation where my volunteerism had begun. I realized that I needed to join a support group which included not only those who were infected, but also those whose lives were *affected* by AIDS. I turned to the AIDS Foundation for a referral to such a group, since the one started by Annette—whom I had met through Carol, my therapist—had been discontinued when Annette returned to school for her master's degree. I joined the support group at the church where our earliest AIDS Foundation meetings were held. It is still going strong, although it has lost hundreds of its members to the disease. I am still a member of that group. I have continued to attend one funeral or memorial service after another throughout the years, as AIDS marches on. To date, two different sources have told me the estimated loss of members of this group is between 400 and 1,200 people. Surprisingly, no such records were kept. In its early days, there were as many as four or five funerals per week for group members who had died. The church installed an elevator to accommodate the many people who are infirm because of AIDS. The dimensions of the elevator were determined by the size of a casket.

As I wrote in the chapter about Jan, AIDS was said to be the gift that keeps on giving. That was supposed to be humorous, but it was said with a seriousness of purpose to encourage people to be aware and alert. It hasn't seemed to have made a difference. New cases are being diagnosed every day. I still hear the newly diagnosed say, "I didn't think it could happen to me."

It was true that my life had become better when I met Jon, as he had encouraged me to tell the group at Rice University, but he moved to San Francisco in 1997. I am invited to visit any time I want, but it is still so very difficult to go back to Gary's city without feeling an overwhelming sense of loss and pain. But Jon and I will stay bonded for the rest of our lives. We agreed to that long before he moved west.

My friend Mark, whom I met through Jon, asked if he would be mentioned in the book, so this paragraph is for him. He didn't qualify on any other grounds, thank goodness.

Many years passed before Truman and I reconnected. We are now in frequent contact, and will always be there for each other, as long as we both shall live. He has had some serious medical setbacks, but is now in good health and is still, after all these years, HIV-negative. When we first began our current relationship, we both couldn't help but notice that we had picked up right where we left off so many years ago. We like that!

Truman still admires the stair rail and expresses his gratitude for Richard's kindness in building it. The stuffed tiger is still on the bookshelf where I had last seen it, over twenty years ago

Bill's parents and I had established a close bond, and every time they sent him a holiday greeting card, including Halloween, they sent one to me with a long note enclosed, and continue to stay in touch. In time, they moved Bill back to Ohio and took care of him until he died. They started a support group similar to the one of which I am a member. I have visited them in their home, and on another trip, to Michigan, when I was visiting my sister, Bea, Bill Sr. drove from Ohio to have lunch with us at the Detroit Institute of Art. I will never forget these wonderful people who were so supportive of their son.

November 19 is the birthday of my friend who died the day before Gary and I went to Club Med. I will always cherish the memories of the lavish Christmas dinners he prepared for his mother and me. Peanut butter soup, roasted duck, strawberry trifle; all were part of his elaborate culinary repertoire. Every year, I phone her on his birthday to reminisce, and to let her know not only that I am thinking of them both, but how much I understand the loss of an only child. She is now in her 90's.

Ken's daughter and I communicate by email. She lives in California with her husband and little daughter, Sophie. I'm very happy to have located her so that we could continue the friendship we had begun when her dad was still here.

Tim's mother has been gracious in allowing me to tell how much her son meant to me, and how he filled my life and home with companionship, joy, and flowers.

On the day Gary left home, to move to San Francisco and start his new life there, just before he boarded the plane he leaned over and whispered in my ear, "Keep on truckin'."

There is an emptiness which no amount of activity or involvement will ever fill. When I first wrote "My heart is rejoicing," I was still experiencing the headiness of accomplishment and friendship. Now it may be time to move on down the road. It will be difficult.